ENTERING ANOTHER'S WORLD

Written by
Margaret Wardell and Robin Thomson

Edited and designed by
David Muir

Contributors
Ruth Batchelor, David Bendor-Samuel, David Burnett, Peter Cotterell, Marjory Foyle, Ruth Giesner, Pauline Hoggarth, John Hollman, Bill Houston, Cathy Humphries, Ken Okeke, William D Reyburn, Bill Roberts, Paul Schrotenboer

Consultants
Hans Breekveldt, John Davis, Peter Haydon, Gordon Showell-Rogers

Cartoons by
Taffy

Published by **St John's Extension Studies**
Bramcote, Nottingham NG9 3RL

© St John's Extension Studies 1994. Reprinted 1996.
  Revised edition 2001.

ISBN 1-900920-01-8

Printed in Great Britain by B&B Press, Rotherham.

Acknowledgements
We are grateful to TEAR Fund for permission to use many articles from the joint Scripture Union/TEAR Fund publication *Prepared to Serve;* and to Scripture Union for permission to use the cartoons by Taffy that accompanied those articles. These articles are all found in boxed pages throughout the text of this book, so that they retain their own individuality and integrity.

We also gratefully acknowledge permission to use material from the following:

- *Student Training in Mission* (STIM), a training manual published by Inter Varsity Christian Fellowship, Madison, USA.

- Material on culture produced by International Student Christian Services, 3 Crescent Stables, 139 Upper Richmond Road, London SW15 2TN.

- *Relate for a Change*, a training package produced by UCCF, 38 De Montfort Street, Leicester LE1 7GP.

- *Readings in Missionary Anthropology* (William Carey Library, 1978), for material on pages 39-40.

- Reformed Ecumenical Council Theological Forum, for material on pages 74-77.

Further copies of this book are available directly from the publishers. There is no extra charge for postage. Cash with order, or telephone 0115 925 1117 for credit card sales.

Also see page 144 for some further resources available from St John's Extension Studies, or visit www.stjohns-nottm.ac.uk for a comprehensive and up-to-date list.

CONTENTS

How to Use this Book

HOW TO USE THIS BOOK

This workbook is designed to help you in the practical task of beginning to live in another culture. It is written for Christians who feel called by God to serve Him within another cultural setting, whether in their own country or abroad.

It is a workbook. That means you are expected to be an active learner, not a passive sponge. Taking time to reflect, talking things through with others, engaging with people of another culture – all of these are important if you are going to learn *how to live* in another culture, and not just learn *about* it.

And it is a beginning. It will not make you an expert. It will set you off on the right road, but culture learning (like language learning) is a life-long task. It requires emotional maturity and perseverance as well as the learning of knowledge and skills. Your ability to cross cultural boundaries will grow as you do.

Three practical tasks are suggested alongside your studies. If you are doing this module with supervision, you will discuss each of them with your supervisor. If not, we still suggest you do them, as they will help you learn so much more. Try to find a mature Christian friend to discuss them with, preferably someone who has lived in another culture themselves.

1. Interviews with someone of another culture
You are asked to make contact with someone of another culture in order to find out what their cultural world is like. You will arrange to meet the person for three sessions, using the guidelines on pages 132-138. It may take time to identify someone and set this up, so you should start thinking about that now. Ideally you should only have your first session with this person after studying Units 1-4, but you can begin any time.

2. Interviews with someone of another faith
You are then asked to make contact with someone of another faith in order to find out what their religious world is like. This might be the same person or a different one. Again you meet for three sessions using the guidelines provided (see pages 139-142). It is best to have studied Units 7-8 before you start these sessions, but again you need to give thought to setting them up well before this.

3. A period of cross-cultural experience
Any period of living in another culture can be used for this module, provided that you spend at least five days there, you live in the same house with people of that culture (family or individuals), and you spend time in daily reflection. If you are going to another culture for holiday/work it will *not* be suitable if you are travelling with friends or a team of your own culture. You must live (or travel) for a five day period on your own or with people of the other culture. You will find guidance on how to 'take the plunge' in Unit 12.

The place could be anywhere in this country or abroad. Some missionary societies arrange short periods of cross-cultural experience abroad, mostly for younger people. There is Christian work amongst people of various ethnic and social groups in Britain. If you are already in touch with a particular church or mission, they may be able to give you a personal contact. Otherwise try an advert in the local press of an area you know is predominantly populated by the cultural group you are interested in, saying you want to be a paying guest for a week to learn more about that culture as part of a learning programme.

If you have already spent time in another culture, you could use that experience provided it was within the last three years and you either lived for at least *two* weeks in the same house with people of that culture or spent more than six months in that culture overall.

If you are doing the module with supervision you will write up your experience into a report for your supervisor. Details of the report are given on page 143. Again even if you are not doing the module with formal supervision, writing a report and discussing it with a mature Christian friend will help your learning.

Other Reading
You can study this workbook on its own without any other books. The module incorporates most of the articles in the TEAR Fund/SU book *Prepared to Serve*, so there is a rich variety of resources here. For a deeper study of the cultural and religious issues we recommend you also read *Clash of Worlds* (Monarch 1990, revised 2001), and you will find specific chapters suggested in the margins of this workbook. You can purchase the book post free from St John's Extension Studies. In Unit 8 you will need a book on other religions – see page 78.

Unit **1**

WHAT IS CULTURE?

CONTENTS

PURPOSE

This Unit will help you to understand what culture is, and how we are all shaped by the underlying values of our culture.

1

A DEFINITION OF CULTURE

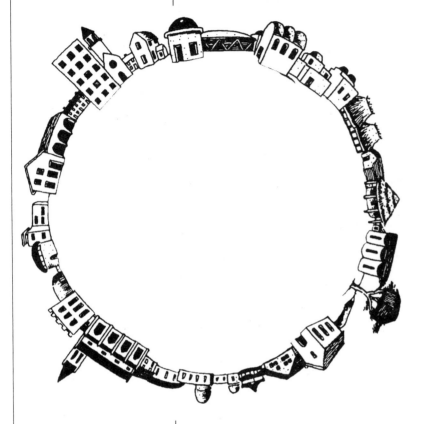

We live in a global village. We can view almost any part of the world at the turn of a switch. We can talk to the other ends of the world in seconds. We can actually cross it physically in a matter of hours.

But although we all live together in one world, it doesn't take long to discover that we actually live in many different worlds. In one way, people are all the same underneath. We share our common humanity. But in hundreds of other ways we are very different.

DEFINITION

It is not very easy to define culture simply. You will find quite a full definition in *The Willowbank Report*, based on a consultation on the Gospel and culture in 1978. The report is also reproduced in *Perspectives on the World Christian Movement*, chapter 20 (Paternoster 1992).

Seeing the Difference

Sometimes it is obvious. When Crocodile Dundee, the Australian hunter, meets the American journalist from New York, it is quite obvious that his rough world of the wild outback has nothing in common with her sophisticated life in Manhattan.

But it isn't always so obvious. The people down my street, or even next door, may live in a different world from me. We have the same kind of houses, go shopping in the same supermarket. But we may have been brought up with different relationships in our family, different ways of eating, attitudes to older people, ideas about what is good, beliefs about life, attitudes to death, family rituals, stories told us by our parents...'

We live in different worlds because we have different cultures or different faiths. Whether the differences are obvious and visible or subtle and hidden, they are very real. And if we want to communicate with people of another culture or faith, beyond the most superficial level, we need to understand those differences. We need to enter their world. Otherwise we will not be able to communicate.

That is what this module is all about. Its aim is to help you to understand and relate to people of other cultures and faiths.

Culture means ...

... the distinct characteristics of a people's total way of life. The groups and institutions of which they form a part cause them to conform to the standards shared by the majority. They over-learn these so that they take them for granted and are not explicitly aware of their operation or even of their existence. They become aware of them only when they encounter someone who breaks them and behaves differently. The host community will consider this behaviour unnatural and illegitimate.

Culture includes ...

Beliefs
These will be about God or reality or the ultimate meaning of life.

Customs
These include behaviour in interpersonal relationships; the way of talking; praying; dressing; working; playing; trading; farming; eating etc. People of one culture may be repelled by a custom accepted in another. For instance, in some cultures belching is the normal way of showing your host that you appreciated his meal, but is thought rude in other cultures. Blowing one's nose in public and stuffing the dirty handkerchief into one's pocket is acceptable in some cultures but repugnant to others.

Values and Ideas
These include marriage, attitudes to death and burial, education, religious ritual, economics. They also include what is true, good, beautiful and normal.

Language
Culture is closely bound up with ways of expression, including proverbs, myths and folklore.

Institutions
These include government, law-courts, temples or churches, families, schools, hospitals, factories, shops, clubs, educational institutions and so on.

■ Culture is shared...
...by a particular group of people having a shared code of conduct, who understand the verbal and non-verbal communications of their group.

■ Culture involves choices
People in a particular society make choices which seem to them to be good, beneficial or true in their situation.

■ Culture is learned
As children grow up they adopt their elders' pattern of life without even thinking about it.

■ Culture is integrated
People need a unified existence. Participation in culture provides them with a sense of belonging, security, identity and dignity. They feel part of a larger whole and share in both the life of past generations and the expectancy of the future of their society.

"Culture when compared to a large and intricate tapestry is made up of numerous threads, larger or smaller, and of various colours, all of which go to make up the overall pattern which in turn serves to interpret any part of it. We are prisoners, consciously or unconsciously, of our culture."

What counts as worship?

Most British people expect to worship in a church with seats and a pulpit, to sing from a hymn-book, to listen to a sermon, to join in prayer, to make an offering. They expect to be greeted by the minister as they leave the service.

But in the Middle East, mosques have no seats and only the men come to worship. In most Hindu temples there is no congregational worship at all. In the Sikh gurdwara men and women sit on opposite sides of the room. In many African churches, people dance and clap, move around and use a lot of symbolism in worship.

People of these backgrounds may not recognise what happens in many British churches as worship at all. They evaluate it this way because of their past experience in their culture and feel it cannot be part of what *they* call worship.

WORLD VIEW

At the heart of any culture is its worldview. This is another key concept that is hard to define. A person's worldview includes beliefs about: ➡

- ■ The universe and how it came to be.
- ■ Supreme beings in the spirit world and their relation with the seen world. The existence of good and evil.
- ■ What happens after death.
- ■ A person's role in their community, society, clan and family.
- ■ Concepts such as salvation.
- ■ A person's relationship to the spiritual world and the natural world.

How does culture work?

In actual practice, a person's worldview affects their beliefs, their beliefs affect their values, and their values affect their behaviour.

But in observing and understanding culture we usually become aware of them in reverse. When we look at people's behaviour we begin to understand their values; by considering values we understand their beliefs; and by considering their beliefs we begin to understand their world view. It is like going back through someone's history – parents, religious authorities, ancient influences on religion – to understand why they think and feel as they do today.

Everyone, religious or not, has a worldview.

- ■ Confucianists view humanity as basically good.
- ■ Christians view humanity as good but fallen, a sinner needing salvation.
- ■ Buddhism teaches that the ultimate goal of salvation is to escape from this world, which is a delusion.
- ■ People who claim not to be religious may have a worldview that sees happiness and self-satisfaction as the aim of life, or serving others as most important.

People may have a different worldview about what progress means.

A Hindu may believe that the universe remains essentially the same while people move through it a life at a time. We grow close to God and escape from life, or sink from one lower caste to another, or even become an animal or an insect as a consequence of the way we have lived our previous lives. The universe does not change or progress.

Behaviour

When we enter a new culture the first thing we notice about people is their behaviour – what activities they engage in, how they dress, walk, greet one another and so on. If we ask one or two of them why they are doing things in a certain way we will receive a variety of explanations, but the most common one is likely to be, "It is the way we do things here." This reply shows that a patterned way of doing things gives people a sense of identity and continuity.

Values

As we continue to observe people we begin to realise that many of their values must be dictated by the similar choices they have made. These reflect cultural values, the next layer of the world view.

If we continued to talk with the people involved, we might find that they had a variety of alternative ways of spending their time. Some may have chosen to study at college rather than become shop-keepers. A woman may have chosen to stay at home with the children rather than go out to work. They chose that particular way because they believed it was the better one.

People make choices all the time. Some walk to work rather than taking the bus, either for their health or to save money. Some people arrive a few minutes early for the meeting because using time efficiently is very important to them. Others may be late for a variety of reasons such as wanting to get another job done first or stopping for a chat with someone they met on the way.

Values are preset decisions a culture makes between choices commonly faced. For example, punctuality has a high priority in Britain; relationships with others take a higher place in India. The values people observe help them to know what they should or should not do in order to conform to the generally accepted pattern of life.

Beliefs

Values in the culture reflect an underlying system of beliefs. In a culture where the education of young people is rated highly it reflects the belief that a person needs to be able to reason and to solve problems. Or it may reflect the belief that education helps you to get a good job, or to escape from village life.

Worldview

At the heart is the worldview, answering the most basic question, "What is real?" This area concerns itself with the deep cultural questions of reality which we looked at above. These questions may be seldom asked explicitly, but culture provides the most important answers to them.

COMMUNICATING

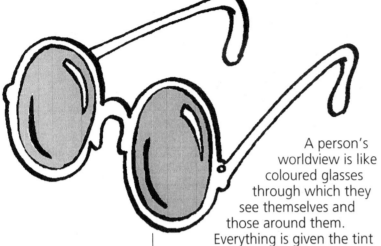

A person's worldview is like coloured glasses through which they see themselves and those around them. Everything is given the tint or hue of those particular worldview glasses. The vast majority of people are used to one pair of glasses from birth and are not predisposed, even if they are able, to lay them aside (even temporarily) to look at the world through a different pair.

If we enter another culture and people respond to the message we give in a different way from what we intended, it does not help them or us to get angry. It only leads to further misunderstanding of both the message and the anger.

People respond to messages within the framework of their worldview. When we enter a foreign culture we need to encode any message with this in mind, and speak within the framework with which they are familiar.

To communicate successfully in another culture we must have an intimate knowledge of the worldview of those we hope to speak to. We must attempt to see the world as its members see it, and experience it as they do.

We have to make a serious effort to understand them and their particular orientation to the situation concerned. We often think we know best how to act, but we must ask whether it is more important to do something our own way, or to build mutual understanding and cooperate

with people of the other culture in making decisions or in carrying out tasks in a way that is acceptable to the culture in which we are living.

Messages sent from our cultural standpoint to people with another, may seem to them difficult to interpret, ambiguous or even offensive. In response they may send us similar messages to which we will also respond differently from what they anticipated. Such confusion can accelerate quickly into a vicious circle of misunderstanding which may result in mutual complaints or accusations or even contact being broken off completely.

This is a particular problem when the two sides have the same linguistic forms and don't realise they are sending an unintended message.

In many Asian cultures the word "No" is rarely used, so that "Yes" can mean "No" or "Maybe". There are many stories of Westerners inviting an acquaintance for a meal, receiving what appears to be an affirmative reply and then being angry when the visitor doesn't show up.

We must be aware of seeming arrogant or annoyed in these situations, and try to find out tactfully where we have made a mistake. We must never ridicule or downgrade other people's views or point out what appear to us to be inconsistencies.

We may have to deal with the misunderstanding but we must do so in a gentle, humble manner, presenting ourselves as learners rather than teachers.

Our first aim should be to build up trust. When we have done this we will find suggestions that we may make or ways to handle situations which are more readily acceptable.

"When you first came I thought you were aloof and superior."

"No, it wasn't that. I was just shy."

"Oh! I didn't think English people were shy."

THE GOSPEL

We also need a good understanding of the meaning of culture if we want to communicate the Gospel effectively across cultures. Everyone has a culture from which they can never totally divorce themselves. However, we can grow to appreciate other cultures and communicate effectively in them if we are prepared to work at doing so.

Sometimes people who try to share the Christian message cross-culturally fail to take into account people's different worldviews and the barriers they cause. They are then disappointed by the lack of genuine change in the other person that their efforts seem to produce.

A Western Christian may share with a Hindu the meaning of Christ's death on the cross. When they receive a positive acceptance to the message they may be elated – only to discover later that the supposed "convert" continues to observe Hindu customs. They had not understood that the Hindu believes in a pantheon of gods, and has simply put Jesus alongside them.

In much the same way a Sikh admires anyone who makes the supreme sacrifice for their faith. Three of the Sikh gurus were martyrs and Sikhs accept Jesus' death as being similar. Only when a person has thoroughly understood that Jesus is unique, can we really assume they have become followers of Christ in the full meaning of the word.

We must present Christian truth within the worldview of those to whom we are talking. Jesus ministered within the confines of the worldview of Judaism. Nevertheless, he adapted his message to the interests, needs and views of his various contacts. He did not communicate with the rich young ruler in terms of the new birth; with the woman of Samaria in terms of

selling what she had and following him; or with Nicodemus in terms of the water of life.

A study of Acts will show how Peter and Paul approached Jews and Gentiles differently when sharing the message of Christ. In no case did they deride or belittle the beliefs a person already had. When we talk to a person of another faith we must be ready to enter into the way they understand religious beliefs before going on to present the Gospel.

In addition we should not major on what we consider the weak points of their religion but also look at its best aspects. We can then go on to show them that Christ offers something even better.

Look at how Peter and Paul adapt their message to the worldviews of their respondents. For each passage write down the worldview of the hearers, and what the Christian message to them was.

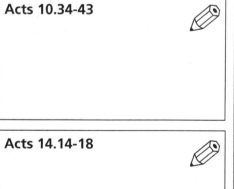

Acts 10.34-43

Acts 14.14-18

Acts 17.22-31

We should honestly and sympathetically deal with the best case that any form of unbelief can make, and then go on to show the deep need that still remains, and how it can be met by the true God and His redeeming son. This is the more acceptable way.
(*World Mission*, Volume 3, *The Cultural Dimension*, page 86)

Read chapter 1. Summarise the four characteristics of worldviews.

Then consider: Why must we take a respondent's view of reality with the utmost seriousness in any discussion?

WHY CULTURES ARE DIFFERENT

'I HAD HANDED HIM THE MONEY WITH MY LEFT HAND.'

David Burnett

It was a typical hot sunny day in Madras as the little taxi hurried through the streets to the church where I was to speak. I had my wife and one-year-old daughter with me. It was a struggle to get out of the taxi with my daughter in one hand and my Bible in the other. Quickly I reached into my shirt pocket to give the driver the necessary rupees. As I handed him the money I saw a look of disgust flash across his face. Then I realised what I had done — I had handed him the money with my left hand. I could only apologise whilst the taxi driver smiled in sympathy at the foreigner. I could almost hear him thinking, 'Why are foreigners so strange?'

Stories such as this could be shared by anyone who has worked in another country for any period of time. They illustrate some of the practical problems of relating to the people of another country. To understand the basic problem it is first necessary to clarify the meaning of the world 'culture'.

'Culture' is a familiar word in the English language. In its popular usage it means good music, art, refined behaviour, and speaking with a well-educated voice. People lacking these refinements are often thought of as being 'uncultured'. For the social scientist such activities are simply elements within the totality of the culture; 'culture' is the total way of life of a society. There are no uncultured societies or individuals. Every society has a culture, no matter how strangely different it may appear to someone from another society. In going to work in another country one will quickly realise the differences that exist, and it is necessary to learn how to work within the context of that culture. This will certainly be a strain to some degree or another, yet it can prove to be one of the most enriching experiences of one's life. Culture generally has six aspects to it.

1. Culture is shared

Culture is shared by a group of people. If only one person thinks or acts in a certain way, that thought or action represents a personal habit, not a pattern of culture. For something to be considered cultural, it must be shared by a group of individuals. For example, an English person shares certain values, beliefs, and behaviour patterns with other English people. These shared customs allow them to predict, to some extent, what can happen in their society, and how they should related to the other people in the group. In so doing, it gives the individual a sense of familiarity with the people, and an identification with that group. It is the shared customs of a society which constitute our main concern and which are called 'culture'.

2. Culture is customs

Culture is rather like the layers of an onion. When one peels off one layer it reveals another, deeper layer. Initially you become aware of many of the outer aspects of the culture of the people, but with time you begin to appreciate deeper aspects of their way of life. The outer layers of culture which tend to catch our attention first are such things as how people dress, what food they eat, the houses they live in, and the way they speak.

Take for example the ways people greet one another. Two Englishmen on meeting would grasp each other's right hand and shake it. In Italy the two men would embrace each other, and kiss each other on the cheek. In India each puts his hands together and raises them towards his forehead with a slight bow of the head. The Japanese would exchange business cards, and give a bow from the waist. All these are different behaviour patterns, but each conveys a similar meaning to the group of people concerned.

In many societies it is common for people to sit on rush mats — which can be a physical trial to those of us used to sitting on chairs! Then there is the matter of eating. Europeans take it for granted that when they sit down for a meal they will be provided with a knife and fork. Yet millions of people find the knife and fork as strange and awkward as we do chopsticks. Some people eat with their right hand, which seems strange to those of us brought up not to touch our food, apart from the sandwich.

British exporters are becoming aware of these and other cultural factors in their overseas trading. 'Getting straight down to business' may look efficient in European and North American countries, but in other areas of the world it may appear crude and distasteful. One must greet the other people properly, and ask about the well-being of their families before turning to business.

Etiquette can be the source of many cultural mistakes. For example the Japanese are often shocked at the loud nose-blowing of the European. It is not considered proper etiquette in Japanese society. An Englishman would embarrass his wife if after a large piece of his favourite apple pie, he failed to muffle his every belch. However, in much of China a loud belch is considered a polite way of saying 'Very delicious indeed!'

3. Culture is language

Language is an important aspect of any culture as it allows the people to communicate between themselves. Thus, learning a language is an important part of being able to relate to people of a particular culture. Yet language is not just a matter of finding the local equivalent to your particular English word. All languages have their idioms and expressions which carry specific meaning. An Englishman speaking to an Indian visitor to this country said, 'I will pick you up at six o'clock.' The visitor was left puzzling over why the man wanted to lift him up from the ground, and especially why he wanted to do this at six p.m.

Culture-related idioms can often lead to misunderstandings. Elijah was driving in Nairobi when he had a slight bump in his car in a parking area. He sought out the owner of the vehicle, and then asked for a message to be phoned to his wife to explain his delay. When he arrived home an hour or so later he found her mourning his death. On the telephone, the message had been conveyed that Elijah had been involved in a car accident. Her immediate question was, 'Is he there?' She was told, 'No.' Her mind was in such a daze that she heard nothing else. Although she spoke in English, she was thinking in Kikuyu. 'Is he there?' meant 'Is he alive?' The reply was intended to be reassuring, in that he was not there but was on his way home. However, she interpreted it as 'No, he's not alive.' She was too overwhelmed to take in anything else.

If the communication of a comparatively straightforward event of a minor accident causing a slight delay was so liable to misunderstanding, we need to be aware of the greater dangers of mis-communications which can occur at other levels.

4. Culture is values and ideas

Customs are the practical expression of a culture, and they reveal the values and institutions of the people — the deeper layers of the onion. At this level are included such practices as marriage, law, education, religious ritual, economics and art.

At the deepest level of any culture is a set of basic ideas shared by the community and fundamental to its whole way of life. These basic ideas are frequently called the 'world-view' of the people, and may or may not be recognised by the people themselves. Almost always these ideas are so 'obvious' that no-one of that society would ever conceive of questioning them.

For example, Western culture never considers the possibility that the material world is anything but real and tangible. People may then ask whether there is anything other than this material world which we can see and examine. However, in classical Indian philosophy the supreme reality is Brahma, and all else is *maya* — illusion. This explains why an Indian guru will spend much time in meditation, because for him the material world is not ultimate reality. By contrast the Westerner focuses attention on the material world, and tends to place a priority on technology and material inventions.

Western people find satisfaction in establishing orderly limits to ideas and daily life. Clarity of thought is for us a sign of intelligence. This is the result of our Graeco-Roman heritage, subsequently fortified by the influence of rationalists such as Descartes and Locke. Ideas must be precise, scrutinised, analysed and classified. By contrast, the Baoule of the Ivory Coast thirst for unity rather than analysis. They desire cohesion, and abhor separating and specifying. They want a unity of nature between man and the supernatural.

During a class on sex education geared to illiterate Baoule, male and female physiology was explained and diagrams and pictures were used to show the development of the foetus. It was all very clear, but at the end of the session the people went away saying 'We saw a lot of things, but that is not the way one has children; there is something invisible behind all that, and that is where truth is to be found.'

It is at this level that religious ideas are of great importance. The Westerner may have great difficulty with the proof of whether God exists, but most societies consider his existence is obvious and without question. Many African societies have a notion of a supreme creator god who for some reason has withdrawn from them. The world is therefore dominated by lesser gods and spirits, and it is to these that sacrifices must be given. Sickness is considered to be the result of affliction by one of these spiritual beings who is wanting to harm the person. Physical causes are not an acceptable explanation of why a person has contracted an illness. The Western doctor may diagnose malaria, for example, and explain that it is caused by a mosquito bite. However, the question that may be asked is: 'Who sent the mosquito?' Someone must have wanted to cause that person ill.

5. Culture is learnt

How is it that the English believe in one way, the Chinese in another, and the Arabs in yet another? Not all the features which are generally shared by a population are cultural. The typical hair colour or blood group is not cultural, and neither are sleeping and eating instincts. Culture is not passed on by genetic inheritance from one generation to another. Rather, it is the process of learning from the previous generation. Sleeping and eating are not cultural actions in themselves because one does not have to learn them, but when and where to sleep and how and what to eat are learned activities.

So a Chinese baby raised in an English-speaking environment will not know a word of Chinese. That may seem an obvious deduction because language is acquired during childhood, but we fail to appreciate the multitude of other factors which are similarly acquired. This allows us to distinguish between what is racial and what is cultural. A child can be considered as having been born cultureless, but quickly begins to learn what are the ways of his or her society. So, even before the child is old enough to evaluate, he is being conditioned, she is being conditioned, by society to speak and act in certain ways.

This process of conditioning continues throughout our lives. Gradually these patterns become the habits of daily life which allow us to predict the behaviour of others, and to concentrate on more important aspects of life. The habits and values which make up culture are passed on from one generation to another. A nomad from the semi-arid Sahel will pass on to his children the skills of looking after their cattle. He will show them how to find good grazing, and to breed the stock. A farmer will pass on to his children the skills of growing crops. The cultural heritage of a people is handed down by the process of subconscious learning and assimilating.

Because most of us are brought up within only one culture we tend to be ignorant of the fact that there are other ways of living. We assume that because we have been brought up to follow certain patterns these must be the best. An Englishman trying to eat with chopsticks for the first time may quickly come to the conclusion that it is better to eat with a knife and fork. Strangely, however, a Chinese lady eating with a knife and fork for the first time will conclude that chopsticks are far better! In fact, both people would with practice develop a dexterity with the various alternative tools, but at first they are strange and unfamiliar. It is therefore easy to make the initial conclusion that one's own ways are better than those of other people. This attitude is found in all societies, and is known as 'ethnocentrism', or more simply 'cultural pride'.

It is not only Europeans who are proud of their heritage – Arabs are proud of their culture, and look back to the time when the Arab Empire was a great civilisation which stretched from Spain across India. Likewise the Chinese looked down on the European sailors as being 'white devils'. Ethnocentrism is a two-way process. We may judge other people's customs as crude, but they may well feel the same about ours.

A Christian working overseas must be aware of the cultural prejudice which is common to us all. Ethnocentrism has an illusive character about it, and although we are unable to notice it in ourselves, those from other cultures find it dominant and often offensive. It can even lead some to argue that not only are their ways best, but as a result their people are best. This is racial prejudice.

6. Culture is integrated

One important aspect of any culture which is frequently overlooked is that it is an integrated system. A people do not just eat in one way, dress in another, work in another, and worship in another without reference to the other activities.

This integrated nature of culture is clearly seen in community development. In 1951 a yellow Cuban maize was introduced into the eastern lowlands of Bolivia. It had many apparent advantages. It grew well in the tropics, matured more rapidly, was less subject to insect attack, and produced a higher yield per unit of land. The new maize seemed to be an excellent means of improving the diet of the people, and it has indeed proved to be very popular – but not for the reasons anticipated. Its very hardness, desirable from the standpoint of storage, makes it difficult to grind, and the people are unwilling to take the time and trouble to haul it to commercial mills in towns. It does however make excellent commercial alcohol, and prices are high. Thus a seemingly desirable innovation promoted alcohol instead of an improved diet.

The 'oneness' of culture needs to be appreciated especially in relation to Christian witness. We cannot simply think that we can replace the religion of people by Christianity without radically affecting the rest of their culture. Their religion is interwoven with the whole culture, and any change will have far-reaching repercussions. The anthropologists are correct when they say that missionaries have changed the cultures of people. The gospel will act like 'salt' (Matthew 5:13), purifying the culture of the people and removing that which is tainted with sin. However, we must confess, with the Lausanne Covenant: 'Missions have all too frequently exported with the gospel an alien culture, and churches have sometimes been in bondage to this culture rather than the Scriptures.'

An understanding of the nature of culture is a long way from providing an answer to all the issues of working in another society, but it will help you in a number of ways. First, it will give you a greater appreciation of why people behave and think as they do. You will see that many of their ways are not so much strange, or primitive, or even wrong, but are just different from yours. Learn to appreciate, and even enjoy these differences. Secondly, it will help you to recognise that you are a product of your own culture. You will then learn more about yourself, and this will help you to evaluate your own lifestyle in the light of the Bible.

Note the six points the writer makes about culture. Summarise them briefly in your own words.

1.

2.

3.

4.

5.

6.

KNOW
YOUR OWN
CULTURE

CONTENTS

PURPOSE

This Unit helps you to understand your own culture and how this affects how you feel about and react to people of another culture.

YOUR OWN CULTURE

Before going to another culture we don't usually think about our culture. To us it is the right way of behaving, and we view other people through the coloured spectacles of our own culture. Only when we enter a different culture do we realise that some aspects of our own culture will offend others.

If you were asked to describe your own culture what would you say? Write down some of its main characteristics:

To a left-handed person like me it was always difficult to remember that eating or giving money with the left hand could cause offence in Indian culture.

A Question of Money

Eleven years after I left India I returned for sabbatical leave. A person from the place where I had worked wrote asking me to bring some presents. I was annoyed by this seeming greediness and thought I was being appreciated only for the goods I might bring. It wasn't until I arrived there and received the warmest of welcomes that I realised that in his eyes I was rich and could easily afford the things he asked for. His request was quite separate from the way he felt about my visit.

The apparent wealth of people can be a barrier to presenting the Gospel if we hide behind our gadgets and financial security. Wealth makes real communication hard, though not impossible.

A Question of Medicine

When I was working in India, I spent some time living in a village with a Canadian and an Indian colleague. The Canadian missionary ran a small dispensary, doling out pills for such simple problems as headaches, worms and so on.

One of her greatest disappointments was to give medicine to a person and find that the next time they came, they had not taken it. Instead, they had resorted to traditional remedies prescribed by the village healer. Many of these involved the use of urine or cow manure, sometimes in very dangerous ways. The village people would not risk offending such a person, for keeping a good relationship with him was more important than taking a Westerner's medicine.

We had been long enough in India to understand their reasoning theoretically but still felt frustrated when we knew ineffective remedies were being used while we had the proper scientifically produced medicines which could deal with the problem. We felt this particularly when a child died of diphtheria after a mis-diagnosis by a quack.

Such a story illustrates how much we take our own culture as the norm and assume people in other cultures will think as we do.

Now look at the following description of nine cultural influences which shape the lives of Westerners.

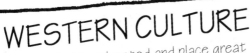

WESTERN CULTURE

- They are highly educated and place great emphasis on using the scientific method.

- They are rich, never having to worry about the provision of life's necessities.

- They place getting a job done above the importance of relationships with those working with them.

- They stress individuality and privacy and believe they have every right to it.

- They have hope. In their culture there are numerous ways of moving out of a difficult situation. Opportunities for education, work and good health are available some provided by the government.

- They try to make their lives as painless as possible. Gadgets for cooking and cleaning, public or private transport for visiting friends and relations, are easily available.

- They are free from the fear of not being able to choose or move when they want to.

- They set individual goals and strive to achieve personal success. They are not easily willing to lose personally for someone else's sake or for that of the community.

- They measure success in terms of money made, objects accumulated, academic honours gained. In a cross-cultural setting they tend to judge their success in terms of wells dug, health lessons taught, churches started.

How accurate do you think this description is? Most of us have been influenced by Western culture, whether or not we were brought up in it. Did you recognise or identify with the features discussed above?

ETHNOCENTRISM

Each of us grows up in the centre of our own world. We are "egocentric" by nature and only as we mature do we begin to break down the circle that separates the "I" from the "You" and to see things from another's viewpoint. We also grow up in the centre of a particular culture and learn its "right" ways. We look with suspicion on other ways and customs, believing them to be improper or inferior. Thus ethnocentrism is based on the natural tendency to judge the behaviour of people on the basis of our own cultural assumptions. (World Mission, Volume 3, page 21).

Hands or Chopsticks?

People who eat with cutlery or chopsticks may be repelled by seeing others eating with their fingers. They may consider scooping up a ball of rice off one's plate and stuffing it into their mouths as uncouth behaviour. But the others view it quite differently. They wash their hands carefully before eating and view the use of cutlery as unhygienic. After all, many different people have had the cutlery in their mouths. But no one else's fingers have been inside their mouths.

To Thank or Not to Thank?

In many cultures the phrase "thank you" is not used. They may laugh at others who use it so frequently. From the standpoint of our culture we may consider them ungrateful or rude when they don't say thank you. But they have their own way of expressing appreciation, not verbally, but by giving a gift as a thank you present when they see the opportunity. We can avoid giving offence by doing as they do, rather than sticking to a verbal thank you. It will take more effort but it will be very much appreciated.

Lazy – or Sensible?

You may know an old song popular in the thirties:

Lazy bones, sleeping in the sun, when you gonna get your day's work done?

The writer evidently thought the other person was time-wasting but "lazy bones" was only doing what seemed right to him in the hot midday sun. What can anyone do but take a siesta? It's only sensible.

The chief danger of ethnocentrism is our pride and attitudes of superiority. It is natural for us to think that our way of doing things is right and proper. Of course others ought to think the way we do. This attitude destroys relationships. To ethnocentric people all other cultures are inferior.

Clash of Worlds

Read the section "Understanding another worldview" towards the beginning of chapter 2. Burnett gives several questions to help identify the characteristic features of a worldview. Think of your own culture (Western or other) and write brief answers to the questions.

Overcoming Ethnocentrism

If we are to identify fully with people of another culture the feelings of "them" and "us" must be conquered. When "they" become part of our circle and we can include them when we speak about "us", we have begun to deal with our ethnocentrism.

Part of the answer to ethnocentrism is to gain an understanding of another culture in terms of its values and assumptions. As we do this we will begin to see its members as valid human beings. Because we are bound by deep-seated attitudes and beliefs, change comes slowly. However long we live in another culture we will always find something new to learn about it.

But we can take some practical steps to hasten this change in our attitudes. For example we can try to identify some of the feelings we have, when we undertake some daily activity in the way the people of the culture we have entered do.

If we know that they turn up an hour later than the appointed time for meetings, we can do the same. It may go against the grain, but we can begin to think through honestly why we feel as we do, and why we attach such importance to punctuality.

We can establish relations of trust with people of another culture by eating with them, joining with them in their leisure activities, giving up some of our naturally preferred ways of doing things and adopting theirs. When we have established trust we will be able to talk with them about our different approaches to living.

Not in a superior "you've got it all wrong" way, but as a humble learner.

A Two-Way Process

Ethnocentrism is of course a two-way process. We may judge other people's customs as crude, but they may feel the same about ours. Making an all-day bus journey with a colleague in India, we took out our lunch-packets which included a hard-boiled egg. As my companion began to crack hers open, a man sitting opposite got up and moved further down the bus. We should have thought through the contents of our lunch-packets before starting our journey. Orthodox Hindus are strict vegetarians and view even eating an egg as taking life.

Racial Prejudice

Cultural prejudice is common to us all. We must be aware of this. Although we are not able to see our ethnocentrism ourselves, those from another culture find it dominant and often offensive. It can even lead some people to argue that not only are their ways the best, but their people are the best. Then it becomes racial prejudice.

Fifty years ago the ethnocentrism of Hitler and Nazi Germany led to the horrors of his attempted extermination of the Jews. But in our own way we can be just as arrogant and contemptuous of other races if we view them as inferior, and a hindrance to getting our own way in terms of how we do things, what privileges we deserve and the respect we expect to receive.

FIRST IMPRESSIONS

By Richard Suffern, on arrival in Kodich, north west Kenya

1. Spectacular scenery, bright sun; different smells, different trees, and nearly everyone is a different colour.

2. Overloaded vehicles. Potholes.

3. Chaos caused by an attempted coup.

4. Even the Third World has pockets of development like the West; more prosperity than I expected.

5. At first, my project colleagues thought that I would solve all project problems overnight. I then had to deal with their disappointment.

6. You may find that you job description differs from what people expect from you.

7. You will find people have no formal education.

8. Many wise people have no formal education.

9. Some missionaries live in more comfortable and pleasant circumstances than they would at home.

10. People's willingness to discuss cheerfully even their hardships.

11. Total lack of modern medical facilities in my vicinity.

12. Local people's inquisitiveness at the arrival of the new white man.

13. Threatening scenes at the site of a minor road accident.

14. People were genuinely concerned that I should not be lonely.

15. Being the subject of jokes that I did not understand.

16. Seventy-six mosquito bites in one night.

17. A different political situation, with nothing but praise for the political leaders in the media.

18. Disappointment on finding the church following a largely Western style of service.

MY CULTURE – AND THEIRS

☞

19. Suddenly having to be jack of all trades, including typist.

20. People's capacity to be content with a little.

21. The educated national thinks very similarly to you in many matters.

22. You need to be ready to work under people who are less qualified academically than you are, and to be willing to learn from anyone.

23. You have to love a people to learn their language well.

24. The best time for evangelising is at the end of a long day's work when you might like to be putting your feet up.

25. You may think that it is better to be young than old. The people you are working with may think the opposite.

26. Hygiene, punctuality, speed and efficiency may be top priorities to you. To your national colleagues, these may take second place behind greetings, hospitality and conversation.

What did Richard Suffern learn about his own culture?

Dealing with our ethnocentrism is an absolute must if we are to establish a relationship of trust with people of a different culture. Only then can we share the Gospel with any hope of being accepted.

Our parent culture not only conditions the things we do but moulds us spiritually, emotionally and mentally. It also spills over into our physical world. Our expectations, dreams, aspirations, value systems, body language, ways of communicating, fears and joys are all culturally discerned. If we do not realise this we will find ourselves very frustrated in another culture. But if we understand how our own culture has moulded us we are much better prepared to adapt to another.

However, this understanding must be used wisely. We must not expect the host culture to change or become like ours. Indeed we must be prepared to let some aspects of our culture go, for the sake of Christ. For example, my Canadian fellow-worker had to forego her reliance on Western science and realise that most village people in India would not risk offending local leaders for the sake of her medicine. Being in good standing with them represented security.

Our cultural difference can also be an advantage rather than a barrier if we use it in a right way. For example, local people may be interested in hearing about the way people do things in our culture – such as shopping, or obtaining water. Even if they find what we tell them unbelievable they will be intensely interested in the actual story-telling and this will create a bond.

The first task we must undertake when entering another culture is to observe its ways. We must not judge the behaviour of the people through the coloured spectacles of our own culture. We should assume that what is being done is normal and try to understand why. Misunderstanding arises out of our ignorance of the new culture.

Within our own culture we are all different. The following exercise may help you to identify some of your own attitudes and responses. These will partly reflect your culture in general but mostly your own particular personality within your culture. Determine to what extent each of the following statements describe your thinking and approach to life. If the statement is not at all descriptive of you write the number [1] in the blank space. If it is very descriptive, write the number [5]. Use number [2] for items that are less descriptive of you, number [4] if it is more so, and number [3] if you fall half-way between.

○ I seek out friends and enjoy talking about every subject that happens to come up.

○ My opinion of myself is determined by what I think of myself, rather than what others think of me.

○ I feel things are either right or wrong. Discussion of "grey areas" makes me uncomfortable and seems to compromise the truth.

○ When I set a goal I dedicate myself to reaching it even if other areas of my life suffer as a result.

○ I tend to associate only with people of the same social status as myself.

○ If offered a promotion which entailed moving to another city I would not be held back by relationships with parents and friends.

○ I always wear a watch and refer to it regularly in order not to be late for anything.

○ When waiting in line I tend to start up conversations with people I do not know.

○ When I hear about a special event taking place I change my plans so I can go to it.

○ Each day I sit down to make a schedule of what I will do that day. I am annoyed when my schedule gets interrupted.

○ I do not take sides in a discussion until I have heard all the arguments.

○ I agree with the statement "the end justifies the means".

○ When involved in a project I tend to work on it until completion even if it means being late with other things.

○ Even though I know it might rain I would attend a friend's barbecue rather than excuse myself to repair the damage a storm has done to my roof.

○ I argue my point to the end even if I know I am wrong.

○ I talk with others about my problems and ask them for advice.

○ I avoid participating in games at which I am not very good.

○ Even if in a hurry while running errands I will stop to talk with a friend.

○ I have set specific goals for what I want to accomplish in the next year or next five years.

○ I feel uncomfortable in discussing topics which are not susceptible to definite conclusions.

When you've completed the exercise, look at your responses and try to think through what they say about your attitudes to life. How much is you, and how much is your culture?

Clash of Worlds

Read chapter 2. (You have already read the first part of this chapter.) Do you think that looking at other worldviews will help us to understand our own better? In what ways?

If you have time, also read chapter 3 which describes the secular worldview.

?

Can you find examples of stereotyped, "ethnocentric" attitudes, on either side of the cultural divide, in the articles on pages 18-20?

HOW OTHERS SEE US

African advice to an English missionary

Once upon a time, I was convinced that every American carried a gun; it was a conclusion I had drawn from TV. So when I went to study in the USA, I asked my fellow students to show me their guns. I was surprised to discover that they did not have any. Thereafter, I was more relaxed in my relationship with them!

Whether we are immediately aware of it or not, the fact is we base our relationships with people from other cultures on stereotypes. Those stereotypes are built up from what we read in books, what other people tell us, and what we see in films and photographs. They may well present us with a distorted picture. So when you come to my country, please be open-minded. The more open-minded you are, the easier it will be for you to unlearn and re-learn.

Based on wide experience of receiving and working with expatriates in my home country, I offer you the following advice. The more you take it to heart, the more welcome you will be and the more valuable your skills will be.

Don't believe everything other expatriates tell you

Some expatriates have come to me and confessed that their colleagues had given them a wrong impression of me. Those expatriates who originate from very conservative backgrounds do not find it easy to relate to those of us in the host country who are quite open and frank. They misunderstand us, dub us as 'stubborn' and 'rude', and destroy our characters before you, the newcomer, have had a chance to get to know us. We must all pray for wisdom so that we know what to tell each other, how to assess that information and what must be found out for ourselves.

Please learn our customs

Some of our ways seem strange to you – but they are not strange to us! There is much that you need to learn, and you cannot learn it at a distance; you must come and live among us. Remember, too, that we still see you as a foreigner; you are always an ambassador of your people, country and church.

The culture in a developing country may be mixed. The European culture seems generally to be more developed technologically and educationally than that of any Third Word country. However, in most developing countries there will be some groups of people who live in a culturally and educationally superior way to some Europeans. In the church, you will find some Christians more mature than those you have left. This leads me to my third piece of advice.

Leave your paternalism at home

Just because I come from what you term an 'under-developed country', it does not mean that as believers we cannot be partners together in God's service. I have known some expatriates claim that they understand the local situation so clearly that they take decisions on behalf of national Christians. This is wrong! The local people will make mistakes. They may ask what seem to you to be silly questions. They may need advice or guidance, but they should be allowed to make their own decisions and should never be manipulated into doing something against their wishes. They should be free to say 'no'.

The apostle Paul was never paternalistic towards the churches he founded. He cultivated a relationship of partnership. They were young churches in need of guidance, but Paul always treated them as self-organised groups and not as groups under his direct personal government. Please do not forget that we have the Holy Spirit of God as much as you do. So seek to build trusting relationships with those you work alongside.

Be careful how you live

Generally speaking, Christian leaders in developing countries believe that Western expatriates come from permissive, pluralistic and material societies. You will often find we are more 'conservative' than people in your country. What you must remember is that people in the host country are watching to see if your behaviour reflects your beliefs. Now if you say you are reaching out to them in love, you will hardly be acting in love if you behave in ways which here are considered offensive, will you?

You must not allow your freedom to become a stumbling-block to others. This is what Paul means when he writes, 'If what I eat causes my brother to fall into sin, I will never eat meat again, so that I will not cause him to fall' (1 Corinthians 8:13). There are two areas of behaviour you should be specially careful about.

What you wear. You may feel like putting on only that which makes you comfortable in hot weather. Here, it may be offensive! We believe that the way you dress says much about you. You must wear enough to keep your body properly covered to maintain our respect and acceptance.

How you deal with hospitality. In England, you probably only ask one question to discover if your visitor would like a cup of tea. In my country you have to learn to persuade people. A conversation may go like this:

You: Zakayo, come and dine with us.
Zakayo: Oh, no! I'm in a hurry. I'll eat another day
You: Come on, Zakayo! Just take a couple of spoonfuls, and then you can leave. We're not going to keep you for long.
Zakayo: No, no! I must go...

And so it goes on. But he does stay, and eats much more than two spoonfuls! Now you may feel he was not telling the truth. But in my country if you say 'yes' straight away it will seem as if you are greedy, especially if you called unexpectedly at the other person's home. And if you only ask once, you will seem selfish and people will think you are only testing them because you do not really want them to eat your food! Such little things may create big misunderstandings and poor relationships.

No matter how much orientation training you receive, there will be situations in which you must seek advice; never be frightened to ask when you are in doubt.

THE WAY YOU DRESS SAYS MUCH ABOUT YOU.

Seize opportunities for witness

I have seen missionaries struggling with words and concepts that are so fragmented that they got lost in a semantic jungle. Precious hours are wasted in debating the difference between 'mission', 'evangelism' and 'witness'. No matter what your profession is, no matter what the goals and objectives of your agency are, you are first and foremost a Christian. And every Christian is a witness, and Jesus said the Holy Spirit would give us power to witness (Acts 1:8).

Most of us believe that mission includes both evangelism (taking the gospel to people) and development (helping with their daily needs so that they can live healthy and fulfilled lives). What people really need is holistic service. It is not enough to be concerned about one aspect of their needs and to neglect all the others. And it is not right to use, say, ministry which addresses people's specific physical needs, as a bait to catch them for spiritual ministry. Remember too that we have to treat all people equally; we cannot give water only to Christians, for example, just because providing a well was a church project; we must give water to everyone because everyone needs it.

Now if you hold these things in their proper balance you can be involved in a physical-needs ministry and yet seize the opportunities for witness. These will arise naturally out of the fact that you are a Christian. A witness simply states what he or she knows or shares what he or she has experienced. A witness is not a judge, however; it is the Holy Spirit who convicts people of sin (John 16:8). Unfortunately, some expatriates with physical ministries lose sight of their primary calling to be witnesses. And to those expatriates and agencies which concentrate on evangelism, we would ask you please to understand that many local churches are committed to development as well; failure to understand this has led to problems in the past.

Tell it the way it is

A few years ago I was visiting the home country of a missionary who was working in my country. He had sent his own people a tape-slide presentation, and I watched it with great disappointment. Its message was fifteen years out of date. When I returned home I asked him why his presentation had not been more balanced. I had to spell out what I meant, because he did not understand me at first. Then he explained that he did not want to take pictures in my country of things which were also available in his country because he thought that only the 'unusual' things would interest the people who sent him. He did not realise that he was very wrong in presenting only the 'unusual'. Please do not present one extreme — be it of wealth or poverty — without also presenting the other.

This is not only important because the people who send you ought to have a balanced picture. It is also important because any nationals from your host country who see your presentation may be very resentful. Some people who have had this experience later try to oppose missionaries.

Some people justify presenting the worst side of things in order to generate sympathy. I do not think this is fair. An honest presentation will generate sufficient compassion from hearts that have been touched by the love of God.

Finally, please be careful what you write about in letters. Check facts and figures carefully. Sometimes, it is better not to write about something until the matter is dealt with. You can leave your readers upset or disturbed because they are so far away and cannot help. However, if you need to write immediately, say to clear up misunderstanding generated through the media, give as many facts and as much encouragement as possible.

A MISSIONARY THROUGH NATIONAL EYES

What we expect from you

- Warm, caring treatment of people.
- Integrity, honesty, humility and hard work.
- An ability to keep confidences.
- Punctuality, responsibility, and respect for others.
- A desire to improve yourself.
- A quiet home and an exemplary family.

What we ask you not to bring

- Prejudices such as expecting to be given certain jobs because you are a missionary, even if you are not skilled in them and there are skilled nationals available.
- The superiority which refuses to accept pastoral help from mature national Christians.
- The bottle-necking of responsibilities by giving them all to expatriates.
- The immaturity which results in selfishness and a lack of sincerity with oneself.
- The tie between your money and your wishes; rather please respect both our dignity and our desires in any giving of money.

CROSSING THE THRESHOLD

Ruth Batchelor

'YOU CAN KEEP THE UMBRELLA. WHAT I REALLY NEED IS SOMEONE TO LISTEN TO ME!'

A tramp, on the move in all weathers, was asked what he needed most. Those who have never experienced the life of a tramp might have expected him to mention food, weatherproof clothing, medicine, drink or a bed. But he replied, 'Someone to listen to me.' Unless we come to love, respect and understand people, we never really cross the threshold into their lives — we are mere observers.

Similarly, development projects can 'scratch where it doesn't itch', because decision-makers (even those with great compassion) normally live outside the immediate problem. So it is essential for development workers to become very close to the local people and to understand their spiritual, physical and emotional needs. People's traditional values and family (and national) loyalties vitally affect their daily lives and attitudes to change.

You discover people's needs only by studying their lives. It helps to spend time living away from other expatriates, in one particular community, getting to understand its way of life. A stay of six weeks (or even repeated weekends) will help you to form good two-way relationships, and vastly increase your understanding. Try to identify with the local people in food and lifestyle. Of course, it is courteous to discuss such visits first with the church leaders and the church you will visit.

The guidelines on page 58 will help you initially to feel the pulse of the community, and to appreciate the skills and wisdom of the people. Enhance their sense of achievement and worth by being interested and encouraging, rather than promising help you may be able to give. Be especially careful not to treat people as if they were just being observed, and do not jot down answers in a notebook. Do this later that day. (Note-taking interrupts both the flow of thought and conversation, and distorts building a natural relationship). Try to learn from each person and build mutual respect. Especially listen, and keep listening.

'Isn't this time-consuming? Is it really necessary?' you ask. That will need to be answered according to the work you are given, your temperament, and your circumstances. But even those tied to a desk, classroom or hospital can make weekend visits. 'After ten years teaching in a Tanzanian college,' an American friend told me, 'I lived for six weeks in a village, and was horrified to discover how much I still had to learn. If I had done that at the beginning, how many mistakes I could have avoided!'

How others see us

The local people may consider us well off and successful. We may even seem to be cocooned by our possessions and resources from the cruel realities of their everyday life. Most of them will have only one good set of clothes — we will have six or more. They will walk to market or church, but we will go by car or motorbike. If we are ill, we may fly to hospital. But what happens to them?

Yet if we are sensitive these resources need not be a barrier between us. It is not what we possess, but rather what we do with it that counts. Invite a group in to listen to your music tapes, or record them singing and play it back. At a special celebration, share your food and home with these new friends.

Be honest about your problems. When you are homesick or worried about the health of your parents or your children, ask the Christians to pray about it. Learning the language can help you make friends, but be prepared for a hard, frustrating slog. Ivan Illich wrote, 'Properly conducted language learning is one of the few occasions in which an adult can go through a deep experience of poverty, of weakness, and of dependence on the goodwill of another person' (*A Celebration of Awareness*). Show appreciation of the help people give you, and, if you become very frustrated by your inability, identify yourself with someone who has even greater reasons for frustration.

Have you ever wondered why Jesus spent thirty years just living in Nazareth before the start of his ministry? Was that time necessary for him? Could he not have cut it short? Yet today, because he lived like that, we know that he fully understands our human life. As Christ's servants, we must try to identify as closely with people as he did and to be as approachable as he was. We need to enter into their ordinary lives, and share with them tears and laughter, failure and success, suffering and hope.

Ronald Eyres, at the end of the TV series *The Long Search*, was asked what struck him most about the different religions he had surveyed. He replied, 'It was the infectious quality of the major religious faiths.' Our Christian faith will only be infectious if we have close contact with God and receive his grace, and also close contact with others to allow that grace to be 'caught' by them.

THE GOSPEL AND CULTURE

CONTENTS

PURPOSE

This Unit will help you understand something of the relationship between the unchanging truth of the Christian gospel and the constantly changing values of the world's various cultures.

WESTERN CHURCH – EASTERN SOIL

I used to worked in a district of North India where there were several groups of Christians, both in the market town which was the centre of the area and the villages around. I saw that the Christians in the town had not only become Christianised but to some extent Westernised.

The Anglican church building in which we worshipped was just the same as those in which I had worshipped in Britain. There was a nave and a chancel. There were pews on each side of the nave, choir-stalls in the chancel, a special seat for the minister, a pulpit, a reading desk and so on.

The only real difference was that we removed our shoes before entering the building and men and women sat on opposite sides of the church.

The service was also very British even though we used an Indian language. The hymns were translations of English ones sung to the same tunes as I had been used to in Britain. We recited the confession and the creed in the form that was used in Anglican churches at home.

The minister dressed in exactly the same robes (except that they were all white).

Why do you think the church and its forms of worship were like this?

(See page 29 margin for my answer)

The Expatriate Christian

Christians who work in another culture are naturally concerned to communicate the good news of Jesus Christ. But often they do not realise that the way they present it may make all the difference to whether its central truths are clearly understood by those with whom they are trying to share it.

Some people fall into the trap of thinking that because they have learnt the gospel within the wrappings of their own culture, that is Biblical culture. This hinders effective communication.

If they are aware of the dangers of ethnocentrism and recognise the need to understand the culture of those to whom they are speaking, their communication will be greatly improved.

If they are aware of the dangers of ethnocentrism and recognise the need to understand the culture of those to whom they are speaking, their communication will be greatly improved.

People cannot think without symbols, so the message must be put in some cultural form to be understood and communicated. We must make every effort not to add our own cultural expression to the Biblical message. Forms and symbols from the host culture must be adapted instead.

How many cultures?

People sometimes think that in order to communicate effectively with another culture, you just need to know your Bible and that culture. Some missionaries have assumed that their task is simply to bring 'the gospel' to 'another culture'.

They do not realise that their experience of the gospel is the gospel *in their culture*. Unconsciously they pass on *that* form of the gospel to the other culture. This especially happens when we assume that our culture is 'Christian' or better than another.

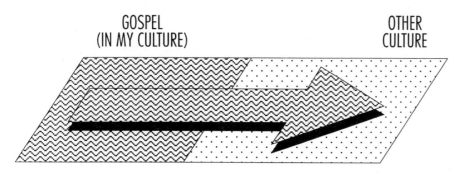

We need first to understand our own culture in order to see how it has affected our understanding of the gospel (and how the gospel has affected our culture). Then we can look for ways to relate the gospel to the other culture as well. So two cultures are involved, *both* in relation to the Bible and the gospel. Some would say three cultures, because the Bible itself comes out of another culture.

We must also realise that the Bible is definite about many moral issues and these principles remain the same in any culture. We must not compromise these and throw out the baby with the bath water. For example, the Ten Commandments apply to every culture. Jesus was the unique son of God and repentance and faith in Him are the only way to eternal life.

However, some Biblical customs such as greeting one another with a holy kiss are inappropriate in a culture where any touching between opposite sexes is regarded as immoral behaviour. When Paul encouraged the believers to do this he was speaking from within the culture in which he lived. When we have managed to eliminate, as far as we are able, overtones of culture in the gospel we present, we can then show the unchangeable values of Christianity that apply in any culture.

Turn to I Corinthians 7.17-19 and Matthew 22.17-21. Each of these passages has obvious cultural features. Take each in turn and decide what three cultures the message moves through. Define the principle being illustrated, and commands being taught in each case. Show how the features of the respondent's culture have been selected and adapted to the situation in question and how the message has been applied in this context.

- How do you explain the fatherhood of God in a matriarchal society?

- Must a polygamist divorce all his wives except one before he is baptised?

- Are the local rites of honouring ancestors a matter of reverence or worship?

Can you suggest other examples of practices (in your culture or another culture) which may be difficult to adopt?

IS "WESTERN" CHRISTIAN?

Not only do many missionaries confuse the gospel with culture, local Christians may be similarly confused in cultures where Christianity was introduced from the outside.

Three Mistakes

Some are under the misapprehension that because Western culture has been Christianised, this is the only form it can take anywhere. Some think that the development of certain art forms in the West is necessarily part of the gospel. A third mistake is to think that since Western culture developed in part from Christianity, this is a perfect expression of Christianity in society.

Many West Indians who migrated to Britain in the fifties and sixties expected that what they looked on as their "mother" country would show them what living as Christians was really like. Most of them expected immediate acceptance in Britain because both home and mother country were "Christian". They were bitterly disappointed to meet rejection and racial prejudice.

Non-Christians Too

People who are not from a Christian background may be similarly confused. One day two Christian women were queuing for a bus in a multi-racial area of Britain. One was English, and one Indian. The Indian Christian turned to a fellow Indian woman behind her and began to talk to her about Jesus. "Oh!" said the woman, "Do you worship Jesus?" "Yes," said the Christian. "So you are not an Indian then?" the other woman replied.

Visitors to Britain also look at our permissive and materialistic society reflected in the media and assume that this is all Christian behaviour. In many countries you must belong to some religion, so they label all Western behaviour as Christian. Because they have a low view of this behaviour they have a low view of Christians, especially any from their own culture. When this happens we need to ask ourselves whether they are rejecting the foreign cultural load which is placed on the message rather than the message itself.

What's in a Name?

Many new Christians have felt obliged to change their name, sometimes choosing a Biblical name, but often a purely western one. An Indian Christian couple named their son Christopher. When he went to a government school where 99% of his class were Sikhs and said that his name was Christopher Singh he suffered a good deal of abuse from others who felt he was allying himself with the West and trying to deny his Indian nationality.

Wealth and Lifestyle

People can also be alienated by the apparent wealth of Christians who come to their country. They feel patronised as well as resenting the glaring inequality in their financial positions. A lifestyle well beyond the means of those with whom the expatriate hopes to share the gospel can create a significant barrier to it. In countries where many survive on a bowl of rice a day, to live in a well-constructed house, own a car, dress in imported clothes, and enjoy three full meals a day seems like incredible wealth.

This is a delicate subject. A Christian must deal with it not only from the standpoint of his heart attitude but also from the viewpoint of others. We communicate our message as much by our appearance and actions as by what we say. Anything that becomes a barrier to the communication of the gospel must be viewed as a negative fact in the attempt to share Christ with others.

Expatriates may feel justified in maintaining a lifestyle similar to the one they enjoyed in their homeland, even when it is in marked contrast to those around them. Sometimes the physical and emotional health of the family are reasons given for not adapting to a lifestyle which more closely resembles that of the surrounding people. While we do need to preserve our family's health and well-being it is questionable whether a Christian who maintains a lifestyle which stands out in its affluence will ever achieve the identification with the people, which is so essential in communicating the gospel.

We cannot have full control over others' perceptions of us but if the gospel is to be communicated we must address the question of lifestyle. Ideally, we should attempt to adapt as nearly as possible to the economic lifestyle of those to whom we hope to minister.

Of course, we can face this problem in reverse when living in a more affluent culture than our own. How do we adapt there?

UNDERSTANDING AN AFRICAN CHURCH

Ken Okeke

When Paul set out from Antioch on his missionary travels, he had one prime aim: to spread the good news of Christ, and so to make as many converts as possible and establish a local church.

He made no attempt to turn that local church into a homogeneous part of the one from which he started out – nor indeed of the one at Jerusalem where the original converts and apostles met in fellowship. He simply led people to Christ from their former ways. Prayer, worship and whatever other things were relevant to their meeting together were uniquely based on their particular cultural setting.

When Jewish believers from Jerusalem attempted to confuse the church in Antioch with the idea that true Christians must practise Jewish customs, the matter was thrashed out at the council of Jerusalem (Acts 15). It pleased the 'church' and the Holy Spirit that they should not burden other people with an unnecessary load. The Christians in Antioch were free to express their faith within their own cultural setting, so long as they were not idolatrous or immoral.

That principle should be followed in every age, and it forms the foundation for understanding any national church. By 'national church' I mean a church that exists within a national boundary, not necessarily a church of that nation in the sense of the Church of England or Church of Ireland. Many Third World countries were 'mission areas' and therefore received missionaries of different and at times divergent callings. The result was that several different churches were planted, each claiming dominance to truth and practice within one country. No one church (except perhaps in India in recent times) can claim to be 'the church' of that country. The church is the body of believers who all over the world accept Jesus as Lord and Saviour and worship God through him as the only mediator and advocate. Any local assembly, be it in a city or a village, Western or Third World country, becomes the local expression of that universal church.

How churches were started
I come from West Africa and it will be helpful to describe the past and present situation of the church there; it is probably typical of many other areas of the world to which the gospel was taken from the West.

Before the coming of Christianity to West Africa, there had existed some form of religion. It can be rightly said that the African peoples were and still are very religious. Religion, however, is not synonymous with Christianity. The only advantage to the early missionaries in their work of evangelisation was that they met people who were seeking God in very vague and ignorant terms but who did have definite beliefs in gods. Their task, therefore, was something like that of Paul on Mars Hill.

The Church Missionary Society began work in Sierra Leone in 1804, but before then there had been a Methodist as well as a Baptist congregation there, started perhaps through the activities of freed slaves. Other missions followed, such as the Baptist Missionary Society and the Wesleyan Methodist Missionary Society in Badagry, Nigeria in 1842. They preached forgiveness of sins and had converts. They were later joined by the Sudan Interior Mission, the Sudan United Mission, the Qua Iboe Mission and probably some others. All came with the liberating message of Jesus Christ as Lord and Saviour – the Messiah not just for the Jews but for the whole of mankind. Now that made sense and the Africans 'brought it'.

What resulted from these ventures was a mixed bag of blessings. Whereas it was good for Africans to break with the past and embrace this new way, the baby was thrown out with the bath water. The early missionaries were handicapped in that they confronted people whose different cultures and habits they did not fully understand. In many cases they had no time or patience to understand. Something had to be established and something therefore was established.

The church was born and God was praised and worshipped not in the way Africans would have done but in the way missionaries did. Both hymn and tune were as foreign as the 'wonder' instrument that made lovely sounds as the missionary squeezed and stretched the colourful contraption from side to side across his chest. The local instruments were not considered fit for worship. For one thing they produced no music recognisable to the missionary, and for another they did not look refined – and of course God would not have been happy with unrefined things! Native names were abandoned and biblical or European names were chosen at baptism. This had its use and value, but its weakness was in assuming that every native or vernacular name had to do with paganism. This trend is now being reversed.

Not only were names foreign. Church buildings took on the shapes of the architecture found in the missionaries' 'home' countries. Anything that did not look like that was not truly considered to be a church building. This approach unfortunately has not stopped. In time the whole concept of Christianity became encapsulated in the Western culture. To worsen matters, colonialism followed hotly behind evangelisation and at times arrived with it. In many cases this caused mission and government to become inseparable.

Three illusions grew out of the advent of Christianity from the West. One was that Western culture is the only possible form that Christianity can take anywhere because the Western culture is a Christianised culture. The second was that high development of certain art-forms in the West was

necessarily a part of the good news of Jesus Christ. And the third was that since the Western culture developed in part from Christianity it is a full and perfect expression of Christianity in society.

The mission stations were often too closely associated with trading factories and government. Christianity was therefore in danger of – and in fact fell prey to – being associated with exploitation instead of liberation. This mistake was to be costly for the mission and the church in the West. Furthermore, sectarianism was imposed on the countries. Baptists would not have anything to do with Methodists, and Anglicans regarded all the other Protestant churches as non-conformists, while the Roman Catholics regarded all of them as pseudo-Christian, people who must be converted and re-baptised. The Third World was left with a divided church and no cultural identity.

The early missionaries also brought education, but this very blessing was to spark off an explosion which brought about more divergence, religious dissidence and organised syncretism. It is common knowledge that all the independence struggles within the then colonised Third World countries were spearheaded by nationalist figures who were products of mission education. They had been educated and had travelled to the West. They returned and began to question the 'establishment'.

The changes that are taking place

Some national churches are now beginning to reverse the trends. Hymns and liturgy generally are being translated, and at times written, in the local language, although some of them are transliterations and the tunes remain recognisably Western. Serious attempts are being made to write songs and choruses in purely African fashion and rhythm, but this practice has not yet become widespread among the mainline Anglican, Methodist, Presbyterian and Baptist churches.

Many indigenous churches have begun to emerge, and there are different types. One is the kind of indigenous church begun by African Christians mostly influenced by the Evangelical and Pentecostal church planting associated with the USA. Most churches of this type have some acceptable theology and lean towards the Pentecostal or charismatic. The founders are often educated and this is an advantage in church organisation. Another type is often charismatic and founded by men 'full of the

Holy Spirit' who in themselves have little or no education. As the churches grew mistakes crept in which led to problems. Nevertheless they provide some Christian answers for the ordinary Africans who cannot go along with the Europeanised churches. These two types of indigenous church can be called 'Evango-Pentecostal Indigenous.'

A third type of church can be classified as Spiritualist using the term in a different sense from the Western occult group. Having begun from scratch or by breaking away from some other church, many of these tend to possess a shaky and dubious theological base. Syncretistic ritual practices, and prophecies, dreams and visions, all play important roles; authority for some doctrines is often misinterpreted portions of the Bible taken out of context. It is pertinent to note that some clever rogues and con-men and women have begun such churches as a way of making an easy living.

Members of such groups are controlled by indoctrination and in extreme cases by fear. One may argue that these Spiritualist churches do help turn people away from their idols. But in fact this turning away from idols to 'God' is often not essentially different from the common practice in African religion in which one god is abandoned in favour of another believed to be more effective. Thus most adherents pursue a result-oriented followership where blessings are earned by the efficacy of rites, sacrifices and ceremonies – just as they would normally do in tribal religion. The catchment area for these churches is wide and elastic, cutting across social and educational barriers.

So we now have within the countries, the Mainline (Western-origin) churches, the Evango-Pentecostal churches and the Spiritualist churches all claiming to be the right type. Apart from the Mainline churches, the others are all reactions against an 'over-Westernised' church. There are hundreds up and down Africa. They have their uses, their strengths and their weaknesses.

Their strengths lie in the fact that they approach Christianity from an African perspective. They adopt a less formal, more lively form of worship using native music and instruments or a mixture of African and Western instruments like the guitar and drums. On the whole they approach more closely the African culture compared to the mainline churches that have not yet broken from European-influenced liturgy and are very often so distressingly European and dull. The best of them, mainly from the Evango-Pentecostal group, seek to express their Christian faith through indigenous and familiar forms of worship while maintaining a sound theology and doctrine. Their growth rate is phenomenal.

The weakness often identified with the Spiritualistic churches is in the area of Christian scholarship. Many times biblical interpretations and usage are mixed up. There is a neglect of theology, and the training that church workers receive is rudimentary in the extreme. The result is that sermons are noted more for 'heat' than 'light'. Equal weight is given to the Old and New Testaments and the idea that Jesus Christ is a fulfilment of the Old Testament is not clearly understood. It is thus no wonder that sacrifices, polygamy and other rituals are practised. This is very disturbing.

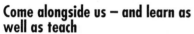

Come alongside us – and learn as well as teach

Any Christian who is going to work in a cross-cultural setting in Africa has to be prepared to take his or her task seriously, and not look on it as an adventure. It is true that Paul and his entourage met some 'adventures' during their journeys, but his letters show that he took his work very seriously and prayerfully.

The churches in these nations have their problems already. In West Africa many of the mainline churches are struggling with how to shed off the European 'skin' and emerge as truly African. The younger people are very eager to see the church become African not only by having African ministers but also by using African-style worship and expression. The older people resist this and there is tension. The problem is that many of the older educated people want to maintain their background, which means their Europeanised education, and church life and style get thrown into the bargain. Some of these people take their churchmanship very seriously, but the danger is that often real Christian commitment is lost in 'efficient' churchmanship. The wish to be seen as different from the indigenous Evango-Pentecostal or Spiritualist churches involves a further embracing of 'Western' church forms and practices.

The dilemma for anyone from the West working with the mainline national church is that you cannot but comply with its wishes and desires. But often the worship patterns are those long abandoned in Europe. You may therefore be tempted to encourage the church at least to move on to what happens now in the European churches whose liturgy and hymns have been modernised. But that will be to start the vicious

circle again. The ideal is for the mainline church to contextualise its worship, but that has to be done very carefully and prayerfully. The cultural patterns must be tested very deeply with the pure gospel of Jesus Christ, for all cultures are earthly expressions of 'being' from people within an environment. And since all peoples are 'fallen', cultures have to be tested to find out which parts oppose scripture, which parts agree and which parts are neutral. This will help churches not to absorb those aspects of culture that originate from a sinful base. At present, there is light in the mainline churches but it is not really burning; it is but glowing.

The best stance to take towards the national mainline churches today is to come alongside them as partners. Then you can advise, lovingly criticise and encourage. The national church needs help to assume a purely national character under Christ without any literal copy-work. Unfortunately some Western Christians equate affluent society with Christian ethics and therefore tend to assume a paternalistic attitude to the national church. Many have discovered through bitter experience that this does not work any more. Even at their own level and within their impoverished circumstances, the faith of these Christians rises above that of many in the established Western churches.

In the other national churches, growth is an accepted norm and many people are turning to the Christian faith from various backgrounds as a result of evangelistic activities. There is also 'biological growth' as populations steadily increase. In the mainline churches, the growth is mainly biological, though there are some

signs that at last something is beginning to stir and new churches are being planted from fresh converts. This move is mainly from the younger members and is a result of the renewal movement beginning to affect the mainline churches. But the growth rate is nothing compared with the Evango-Pentecostal churches.

The churches do need more in-depth teaching and discipleship. More workers are needed to train, prepare and equip the vast numbers coming to the Christian faith. This is probably the task that needs the most attention from the West since evangelising is best done by the local people.

However, teaching, preparing and equipping must be contextualised.

On the whole the African is religious and willing to be shown the Way which is Jesus Christ. He is willing to be taught and he is willing, like Andrew, to go and tell his brother about his new faith in Christ. Generally Christianity within the Third World countries, whether mainline or otherwise, is coming to a level where one is beginning to wonder whether the West will not become the mission field. Perhaps the West can, through interactions with the national churches, re-learn and re-capture this lost quality of excitement in telling the good news. When new life and zeal sweep through the flagging churches of the West once more and children of God are moved around from west to north, south to east, Western to national and vice-versa, the world may yet again begin to hear it loud and clear that Jesus saves!

SYNCRETISM

In attempting to clothe the Christian message in the culture of the people we must be careful not to fall into syncretism.

Being Cultural

Occasionally a cultural form or symbol from a non-Christian setting has been adapted to Christian expression without those who have done so realising that it has carried with it the meaning attached to it in the former belief system. These old meanings can sometimes distort or obscure the intended Christian meaning. For example, think of some of the symbols attached to Christmas in many cultures.

Being Foreign

On the other hand, some Christians have been so afraid of syncretism that they have not adopted any local cultural forms for the gospel. So it has remained "foreign". Any attempt to adapt the gospel to a culture must be done very carefully. Some understanding of the religious background from which a convert is coming is essential; as well as some understanding of how and why certain symbols and forms are used in his former religion.

A Tragic Vacuum

Most cultural forms meet a need and perform an important function which contributes to a culture's existence. When it is scattered or eliminated care must be taken that a vacuum is not left. A cultural substitute must be found, otherwise the result may be tragic. In some parts of Africa where polygamy is practised believers are asked to give up all but one wife. Satisfactory arrangements must be made for the others. In some instances this has not been done and without means of support they have been materially deprived. Some have even ended up as prostitutes or slaves.

How can I, who have been born and brought up in one culture, take the truth out of the Bible, which is addressed to people in a second culture and communicate it to people who belong to a third culture, without either falsifying the message or rendering it unintelligible?

In "Understanding an African Church" (pages 25-27) Ken Okeke gives examples of the way the gospel was seen in a Western cultural form. Note the attempts to reverse this. Which are more effective? And why?

We may sometimes feel helpless. However hard we have tried to dissociate the Christian message from one particular culture, we must leave the result to God. If not, our tensions and sense of uncertainty about whether we are failing or succeeding will make the message less powerful.

Let us remember that the same Holy Spirit who guided the original authors of the Bible, will help us to interpret it and show us points of empathy with believers and unbelievers through which we can minister Christ to them. He will do his own work in the hearts of our listeners. We are not responsible for convicting them, that is the Holy Spirit's work. When we have done the best of which we are capable we should leave the results in God's hands.

A Rural Experience

In contrast to my experience in the Indian town which I related at the beginning of this Unit, I also have some experience of what can happen when Christians are free to do their own thing without the influence of another culture.

In one of the villages where I spent some time, the local Christians decided to build their own church. They were poor and limited in both resources and experience and the building work took a long time.

But when it was finished it couldn't have been more different from the town church. It consisted of one room, square in shape, with a mud floor coated with a mixture of cow dung and mud which all the villagers used in their homes. (Contrary to what you might expect this does not smell, and it can be polished to a high shine). The roof was also made of the thatch used in the village houses. There were no seats, no pulpit or reading desk.

The worship was led by some of the village men except when a minister was able to come out from the town. It was simple and dignified and reflected the faith of these village Christians.

What things from the list below, do you think would be most likely to lead to syncretism? Which could be used to contextualise the gospel in that particular culture? Explain your answers, in a sentence or two.

> Traditional sacrifice of a pig or chicken before a wedding ceremony.

> Using national rhythms and melodies for hymns and choruses.

> Painting pictures of Christ that look like one's ethnic race.

> An all night gathering in the home of the deceased nine nights after his death.

MY ANSWER
to the question on page 22

One reason is that the church was built during the British Raj. The people at that time saw that style of church as the "right" one for worship. It fitted into their culture. As I look back I feel sad that my forebears had given the impression that Christian worship was inseparable from Western culture. They could not imagine, perhaps, that people could worship in any other way. It is easy to see their mistakes. It is not always so easy to see our tendencies today to confuse the gospel with culture.

Read chapter 14. We shall return to this later, so you do not need to try and understand everything at this stage. But notice the examples Burnett gives of the questions which arise when we try to identify cultural practices which are appropriate for Christians.

Read through the following list of statements related to Christian living, and determine which is a cultural value [C] and which is a Biblical value [B]. Write the letter [C] or [B] before each statement.

For example:

[C] To be prompt at every meeting and appointment.

[B] To be prayerful.

◻ To line up when paying for the bus or for food.

◻ To make sure you telephone before dropping in at a person's home.

◻ To send thank you cards.

◻ To express directly your feelings. "Tell it like it is"

◻ To be honest.

◻ To have wine at communion.

◻ To think of others before myself.

◻ To support my parents materially and in every way I can.

◻ Everyone is entitled to freedom and the pursuit of happiness.

◻ Save up for your retirement.

◻ Respect the elders above you.

◻ God helps those who help themselves.

◻ Greet each other with a kiss.

◻ Have a church building.

◻ Cleanliness is next to godliness.

◻ Do things decently and in order.

◻ Drums, Pianos, Guitars – any musical instrument – can be used for worship.

◻ Little children should have their own church.

◻ Democratic process.

◻ Practise hospitality.

◻ Give to those in need.

◻ Capitalism.

◻ Food for everyone.

◻ Don't go to court to settle issues between Christians.

◻ Honesty.

◻ Prevent people "losing face".

◻ Saying grace before meals.

◻ To congregate for "a time of worship".

◻ Favouritism shown to fellow Christians. (E.g. supplying them with a job).

◻ Denounce bribery.

Think again about Paul's sermon in Athens, and his approach to communicating the gospel. In what ways did he show sensitivity to his listeners' situation? (Acts 17.16-34)

If you have questions about some of these, write them down here and try to discuss them with some friends.

ENTERING ANOTHER CULTURE

CONTENTS

PURPOSE

This Unit will help you appreciate what is involved in beginning to live in another culture, what can be achieved and what in most cases cannot.

LEARNING LIKE A BABY

We are not ready for the challenge of cross-cultural ministry until we are willing to give up our inherited ways for a time and begin to learn as a child.

INTERVIEWS

At this point you should have already made arrangements for your interviews with a friend from another culture. If you have not done so, please do so at once. You will find the guidelines for the interviews fit well with this Unit of study.

As you begin meeting with your friend you will find that it greatly enriches your understanding of the Units which follow.

Before we go to another culture we may have pictures in our head of what people are going to be like. Though it is good to prepare in every way we can, we must not form a stereotype and expect all of "them" to behave in a certain way. Nor when we arrive should we pass judgment on first impressions.

One lady I know says, "I know whether I'm going to like people the instant I meet them." As a result she often dismisses people out-of-hand without ever discovering what they are really like.

It is also possible to label people as "ungodly" because they don't have our priorities.

Are we prejudiced in favour of those who are good timekeepers or those who are not? Our answer to the question may not necessarily be God's. No culture has God's priorities perfectly. In His scheme emphasis on time and availability for people exist together in complete harmony.

We must adapt to the priorities, especially of time and event, of the people with whom we work. Some expatriates are blind to this and continue to reflect their own cultural

priorities in the circumstances where they are now living. But God commands that we do nothing out of self-centredness and satisfy the priorities of others before we consider our own.

Culture is always learned and shared with others. In the process people begin to perceive and respond to each other in culturally different ways. The mind will screen out information that is perceived as not essential and protect us from emotional and intellectual overload. Nevertheless, attempts to belong to a group whose standards are in conflict with our own does produce some emotional stress within. We have to begin to learn all over again like a child and grow in the middle of the new culture.

> **We have to be learners and let the people of that culture teach us, before we can teach them.**

And when we do teach we must do so in the spirit of Christ.

To some Christians setting aside one's national identity or one's church or social identity may seem like sacrilege. Such people assume their way of living is equated with "godliness" and defend its apparent rightness. But Jesus Christ did not cling to the nature of God. He became not only a Jew but a servant among the Jews.

The Model of Jesus

Jesus Christ is the only faithful example of divine love in interpersonal relationships and communication. He brought the reality of the love of God into human experience. What did this mean for him?

When we need to adapt to another culture we can appeal to God for help. For He has been through such an experience Himself at the very deepest level.

■ **He came as a helpless baby**
Not as a fully developed adult expert or as part of a ruling class. He was born as an infant in a humble family, in a conquered land.

■ **He came as a learner**
He was not born with a knowledge of the Jewish language or culture. He learned to speak from his parents, his trade from his father, the scriptures in worship from the synagogue leaders. He studied Jewish culture and lifestyle for 30 years before beginning his ministry. He knew about life and its problems. Philippians 2.6-7

tells us that he was in very nature God who took on Himself the very nature of a servant and was made in human likeness. He called himself the Son of Man, so identifying with those to whom he was sent.

■ **He left the glory of heaven**
He became a vulnerable, dependent human being (see Hebrews 2.17, Isaiah 53.3). He knew hunger, thirst, poverty, oppression, rejection and loss. He wept over Lazarus, agonised in Gethsemane. He came to know human nature internally so he had tremendous insights in ministry.

To become incarnate in another culture and in the lives of the people to whom we have come, we too must begin as children, growing up and learning as Jesus did. We must be learners as he was, letting others teach us how to behave as they do.

To follow the example of Jesus means undergoing drastic personal and social re-orientation. We have to reassess and modify our values and behaviour, in the matter of time and schedule particularly. We have to develop new strategies for living. All this will cause us stress. We will also probably experience guilt and frustrations over our failure to live up to the values instilled in us by our native culture. At the heart of this issue is the question of submission to God, and His will for us – to consider others better than ourselves and to yield to those whom we have to serve.

WHAT ARE CHRISTIANS _FOR_?

Peter Cotterell

For the first four years of my life as a Christian I knew what I should not do, but I did not know what I should do.

My parents were not Christians. They never went to Church, I don't think they ever prayed, and so they could not show me what a Christian should do. The church that I went to all those years ago did not help much either. They made it quite clear to me that I should neither drink alcohol nor smoke, go to neither the theatre nor the cinema, never dance — and if I did, I should not be caught. I should not wear bright-coloured ties, thick-soled shoes or fancy suits, or long hair. But everything was negative.

Then a young lady joined the church, and strange stories began to circulate about her. Before the Sunday evening service, she was on the streets handing out tracts and inviting people, _any_ people, to come to church. Odd! After the service she was out there again, this time inviting young people to some kind of a service in a nearby bungalow. Odder still! Apparently it was not unknown for her to march into the queue at the local cinema, pass out invitations and then march off with some of the people — and apparently some of them actually became Christians. The church, I remember, was not amused, certainly not impressed. It was embarrassing! They had never gone in for that kind of behaviour before Geraldine came.

I was perplexed. I thought it over. Surely she was right. No-one had come looking for me, but if they had... maybe I would have found the way to God much more quickly. I could not see anything in my Bible that was against what she was doing. In fact it looked to me as though Geraldine was simply following the example of Jesus. So I joined her. And eventually we joined up for good... but that's another story!

I soon realized that what the church was doing _inside_ the church was good, and that

what Geraldine was doing _outside_ the church was also good. In and out we were doing what God wanted us to do. I had two answers to the question 'What is the Christian supposed to be doing in the world?'

Not long after this I faced the even bigger question: what was I going to do with the remaining fifty or so years that God might allow me to have down here? There were many possibilities. Once I became a Christian I discovered a love for study, so I could be a student. I was always a talker, so I could be a teacher, or a politician. I was good at mathematics so I could be a tax inspector or a milkman. I was very fit, so I could be a postman. Here I learned a very important lesson: I could be any of those things and still be doing in this world what God expected a Christian to be doing.

In fact I did some of those things. I was a student, and other students became Christians too. I was a schoolteacher. A few years back a man came up to me at church one Sunday, and said, 'You don't remember me, do you?' He was right; his name rang no bells. 'You taught at the school when I was in the fourth form, and you were the first real Christian I had ever met.' I was also a Christian postman, and discovered very quickly that behaving in a Christian way did not make me very popular. But it did make new Christians.

Eventually I became a missionary, in Ethiopia. But still it took me a long time to discover the next part of the answer to my question 'What should a Christian be doing, here on earth?' Some people seemed to think that the answer was 'Be a missionary'. And I nearly fell into the trap of believing that what Christians ought to be doing here on earth was to be missionaries. Which would have been silly, because I discovered that missionaries dug gardens, posted letters, built schools, taught arithmetic lessons, performed operations, ran printing presses and balanced the books at the end of the month just like the people back

home. Oh yes, and we preached sermons and translated the Bible, and had prayer meetings. Really, missionaries just did a selection of the jobs which other people did all over the world.

Well, some of them did. Some of them were different. I could see that. Some of us wore the label 'missionary' very prominently and then got on with the job of living our lives much as anyone else would. But some were not too worried about the label 'missionary', and in fact some of them were not some of us at all. Christian doctors working in the government hospitals, for example. Nurses. People who came out to help when the famines first began to hit Ethiopia. Schoolteachers.

Everyone seemed to know that these people were different. A doctor regularly had long lines of beggars outside his home on Sundays, because he handed out free dinners. A pilot kept bringing people to me because their marriages were in a mess and he thought that I could do something to help. An oil expert helped set up a kind of soup kitchen for the hungry. Another doctor had an enormous Sunday School in her home; her friends ranged from princesses to shoe-blacks (I know because they all turned up for her funeral in Addis Ababa!). And from them I began to add more pieces to my picture of what a Christian ought to be doing in this world.

And when I came to fit it all together, I discovered in my simple way that my task, my job in this world, was to live like Jesus.

Live as Jesus lived
So far I have quoted no texts, and made no references to great theologians or even to recent arguments about the nature of Christian mission. I have just told how I gradually came to discover what I ought to be doing in this world.

But someone else could easily disagree with me and say that Christians ought to shut themselves up in monasteries, or go to Bible College, or get into politics. So I do need to say that when I look at the Bible I discover that my idea of what

Christians ought to be doing here on earth is not so far out. Jesus appeared to his eleven apostles on resurrection Sunday and he gave them their orders: 'As the Father has sent me, I am sending you' (John 20:21). Actually they had heard those words just a few days earlier, when Jesus was praying: 'As you sent me into the world, I have sent them into the world' (John 17:18). So Jesus wanted his followers to go into the world just as he had done.

Now we have to be careful here. Muslims believe that they should live as Muhammad lived. Many of them take this to mean that they should dress and eat like Muhammad and generally do or not do what Muhammad did or did not. Great volumes of Traditions have been produced to tell Muslims just how Muhammad lived. But Christians do not copy Jesus' clothes or eating habits, although we do live as Jesus lived.

We find Jesus taking time to be with children. We find him feeding hungry people. We find Jesus healing those who were ill. He seems to be much more often with poor people than with rich and important people. We find Jesus praying. We have an account of one of his sermons in the synagogue at Nazareth. We find him speaking out against hypocrisy, especially religious hypocrisy. He had some remarkable friends, but he also made many enemies. Jesus was not a particularly comfortable person to have around; he was unpredictable. And he was clearly a person of power.

In fact Jesus lived a very full, diverse sort of life. It was not all preaching, or all praying, or all healing, or all feeding the hungry. And I can be living like Jesus when I do any one of these things. But Jesus lived this way because he thought a certain way. He showed that he had certain beliefs — and I mean *certain* beliefs.

He believed in life after death and he believed in judgment. He believed in repentance. He also believed that God was King of the Universe and he talked a great deal about God's kingdom. Jesus believed in Satan, the deceiver, the tempter, and he believed that there was a satanic kingdom against which he battled. Jesus believed that all the rest of us were prisoners, slaves to sin, and it was his task, and his alone, to rescue us; he called it 'ransoming' us. Now all that makes up the 'world view' of Jesus. And it is a person's 'world view' that really determines his or her behaviour.

If you think that there is no life after this life, no God, no judgment, then that will affect the decisions you make about how you live. Like Stalin you might feel that the massacre of

INSTRUCTIONS
1. Live like Jesus

hundreds of thousands of peasants did not really matter; they were, in his view, just higher beasts. If like the Christian Scientist you think that suffering is an illusion, then you will not be much worried about pain and hunger. If like the Hindu you believe that today's suffering is simply the fair consequence of your own sin in a previous life then perhaps you will not worry too much about starving, homeless people in Calcutta or Bombay.

So the Christian shares the 'world view' of Jesus. I believe in two kingdoms, the kingdom of God and the kingdom of Satan. I believe that people, some of them my own neighbours, are prisoners of that evil world, and yet they do not know it. I believe that some political systems, perhaps most, are manipulated by Satan's kingdom, and stand against God. And because I believe as Jesus believed I live as Jesus lived. That is my mission. If you want to have it put theologically: I believe in incarnational Christianity.

That means Christ was God-in-human-form, 'God incarnate'. He was God living among us in the way in which we should all be living. He knows, therefore, exactly what this world is all about. And before he went back to his Father he said that he was sending me into the world just as his Father had sent him into the world. So Christians are expected to be a sort of on-going incarnation. We should all of us be doing today what Jesus did when he was here.

The consequence should then be that other people will start living in the same way. And that seems to be exactly what Jesus had in mind when he gave his apostles their orders, in what has come to be called the 'Great Commission': '... go and make disciples of all nations... teaching them to obey everything I have commanded you.' Matthew 28:19,20

Jesus did not tell his apostles that they were to produce church-goers or even converts. What Jesus wanted was 'disciples'. Disciples are people who live in the same way that their teacher lived.

In fact it is worth noting that very early on the Christians were called people of 'The Way', probably not more than a couple of years after Jesus' resurrection. In Acts 9:2 Saul of Tarsus gets permission to arrest and imprison anyone 'who belonged to the Way'. In Acts 19:9 we read that some of the people of Corinth 'refused to believe and publicly maligned the Way'. And again in Acts 19:23 we hear of 'a great disturbance about the Way'. When Paul was arrested in Jerusalem he admitted to the mob there that he had 'persecuted the followers of this Way' (Acts 22:4). Christianity was very quickly seen as a whole Way of life, not just a collection of theological beliefs, not just a creed. Those first Christians produced the People of the Way.

This is important. The mission of the church today is still the same: to produce People of the Way, people who live differently. Not necessarily people on a church roll, not merely people who have been baptised or who have signed a form or recited the creed, but people who live a certain way.

Christians have their roots in Judaism. The Jews had no nonsense about part of life being religious and part secular, part spiritual and part material. Every part of life was religious, every part was spiritual. Most of us in the Western world have forgotten that. We think that going to church is religious, but going to work is secular. We have got it wrong: everything the Christian does is religious. Every sentence we speak, by its choice of vocabulary and its intonation and its intention, is spiritual. If we are selling soap powder there is a Christian way to do it. If we are driving a bus, there is a Christian way to do it. We are People of the Way. Our mission is to follow the Way and to lead other people to follow it.

Act as Jesus acted

But are there priorities? Are some parts of our job more important than other parts? I used to think so, but now I am not so sure. You see, I have lived through the Ethiopian famine, where the priority *had* to be feeding the hungry. But I recall an appalling plan crash in Addis Ababa, which left the dead and dying strewn over a field near the airport, and there the priority was to speak a word for Jesus.

The priority, I have decided, is quite simple: it is, in every situation, to do what Jesus would have done. Well, not quite; after all he was the uncreated Son of God and I am a bought-back part of his creation. But still, I want to be like Jesus to the people I meet every day.

There is a little phrase in the New Testament which is very much misunderstood, but which explains what I mean: the phrase 'in my name'. Jesus used it about giving someone a drink (Mark 9:41) and about welcoming little children (Matthew 18:5), and Paul used it in his letter to the Colossians: *'And whatever you do, whether in word or deed, do it all in the name of the Lord Jesus.'* Colossians 3:17

Now neither Jesus not Paul meant that whenever you gave someone a cup of water to drink you should solemnly intone the words 'In the name of Jesus'. What they meant was much more simple and yet much more profound: do it *as Jesus would do it*, as if Jesus were *your* name.

I do not think that we should try to identify priorities, as though it were more important to preach a sermon than to hand out a sandwich. Handing out sandwiches may have remarkable spiritual results. In Ethiopia I went with a relief team into the famine area. In our huge truck, loaded with emergency food, we drove into the market area of a town in the north of the

country. There we were to unload and pack the food up into the mountains beyond to feed the starving.

But when we stopped the truck we were at once surrounded by an enormous crowd of people: hundreds, thousands, perhaps. I was a little bit afraid. I spoke to those nearest to us, and at once they realized that I could speak their language. The word swept through the crowd, and they began to demand that I teach them about Jesus. They could not make us out, you see. They knew we were Christians. They were Muslims. But it was we Christians who, in the name of Jesus, had come to feed them. Their own people had not bothered. Why had we? Why did we feed them, not asking who was Muslim or who Christian? Had I tried to preach in that market place a couple of years earlier I would have undoubtedly have been in danger of my life. But there was a time to feed the physically hungry, and there was a time to feed the spiritually hungry. Priorities had changed and *now* was the time to preach. I preached. That is what Jesus would have done.

My mission, my task, the reason God has left me here, the task of the church, is to live like Jesus.

Study prayerfully Philippians 2.1-8, and think through what being incarnate in another culture means to the Christian.

There are two major truths we must accept without reserve:

1. God made us, and whatever He does is for our own good. Our life history, our personal trials and experiences, weaknesses and strengths are what God is going to use to continue His creative work within us. If we don't accept the goodness of His past dealing with us, we will probably not trust Him for the future.

2. The host culture, like all cultures, including our own, is a valid, though imperfect way of life. To become incarnate in another culture does not demand loss of moral integrity. Jesus was fully incarnate in Jewish culture yet without sin.

Write a short paragraph entitled "The cost of living as a Christian in a foreign culture".

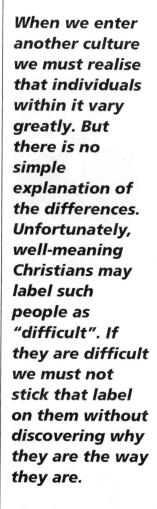

When we enter another culture we must realise that individuals within it vary greatly. But there is no simple explanation of the differences. Unfortunately, well-meaning Christians may label such people as "difficult". If they are difficult we must not stick that label on them without discovering why they are the way they are.

IDENTIFICATION

The keys to our growth and maturity in a cross-cultural ministry are incarnation and dependence on God. Our job in this world is to live like Jesus. In the process we need to learn to understand people from within – their spiritual experience, physical needs, values, family and national loyalties. These all affect their daily life and culture.

The First Steps

The relationships we build up in the first few days of being in the different culture are particularly important. They can have a critical influence on the whole process of identification and incarnation. The unconscious attitudes formed at this early stage could well determine the effectiveness of the entire period of service in that culture. In some countries new arrivals spend the first six weeks living with a local family. Anyone going to work in another culture should consider doing this at the outset of their time there.

> **Identification is not so much adapting to this or that kind of dress or food but entering into the experience of other people with understanding and taking their worldview seriously.**

A Friendly Distance

If we feel that we are a different kind of people from those with whom we work, this will communicate itself to them in many ways. We may live apart from them, allow them only into our living rooms and not permit our children to play with theirs. When we identify with them it will be in formal ways – at an annual feast, at our place of work, in their homes if we are formally invited, on committees. We may wear national dress on certain occasions but keep people at arm's length. These things stress the differences between people and demonstrate how superficial is the desire for unity that we may express in words.

Are We One of Them?

The real test of identification is how we handle informal times and our most precious personal belongings. When the committee meeting is over, do we go aside with other expatriate colleagues to discuss photography?

The basic issue is not living in the same type of house, eating the same food or wearing the same dress. We can do all these things and still communicate to people that mentally we are different. The issue is our basic feelings. If we see and feel ourselves to be one of them, it will come through even if we have a different lifestyle. It is not a question of formal equality but true love and mutual reciprocity.

Being Like Christ

A sense of oneness with people creates in us an interest in learning more about them and sharing in their culture. Because of His love Christ became incarnate in order to bring us God's good news. We need to do the same if we are to expect people of another culture to take what we say about our Christian faith seriously.

Not everyone is cut out for living in and identifying with another culture. Those who go must be ready to change habits and lifestyle preferences. Some may be called to embrace poverty. The degree of identification achieved and the role they take will have a tremendous impact on their potential for sharing Christ effectively. They must be innovative but also unjudging. Above all they must be believers who are committed to a demonstration of God's love in relationships.

In "Ownership of a gun" (page 39), what happened to "William Reyburn" in order for him to become "Obam Nna"?

Can you think of other examples of limits to identification? (see page 40)

OWNERSHIP OF A GUN

William D. Reyburn

Living in an African village caused us to become aware of the effect of other formative attitudes in our backgrounds. One of these in particular is the idea of personal ownership. While living in the South Cameroun village of Aloum among the Bulu in order to learn the language, we were received from the first day with intense reception and hospitality. We were given Bulu family names; the village danced for several nights, and we were loaded with the gift of a goat and all kinds of tropical fruits.

We had been invited to Aloum, and we were not fully prepared psychologically to understand how such an adoption was conceived within Bulu thinking. Slowly we came to learn that our possessions were no longer private property but were to be available for the collective use of the sub-clan where we had been adopted. We were able to adjust to this way of doing because we had about the same material status as the others in the village. Their demands upon our things were not as great as their generous hospitality with which they provided nearly all our food.

Then one night I caught a new vision of the implication of our relation to the people of Aloum. A stranger had appeared in the village, and we learnt that Aloum was the home of his mother's brother. It was the case of the nephew in the town of his maternal Uncle, a most interesting social relationship in the patrilineal societies in Africa. After dark when the leading men in the village had gathered in the men's club house, I drifted over and sat down among them to listen to their conversations. The fires on the floor threw shadows which appeared to dance up and down on the mud walls.

Finally silence fell over their conversations, and the chief of the village arose and began to speak in very hushed tones. Several young men arose from their positions by the fires and moved outside to take up a listening post to make sure that no uninvited persons would overhear the development of these important events. The chief spoke of the welcome of his nephew into the village and guaranteed him a safe sojourn while he was there. After these introductory formalities were finished the chief began to extol his nephew as a great elephant hunter. I was still totally ignorant of how this affected me. I listened as he eulogised his nephew's virtue as a skilled hunter. After the chief finished, another elder arose and continued to cite cases in the nephew's life in which he had displayed great bravery in the face of the dangers of the jungles. One after another repeated these stories until the chief again stood to his feet. I could see the whites of his eyes which were aimed at me. The fire caused little shadows to run back and forth on his dark face and body. "Obam Nna," he addressed me. A broad smile exposed a gleaming set of teeth. "We're going to present our gun to my nephew now. Go get it."

I hesitated a brief moment but then arose and crossed the moonlit courtyard to our thatched-covered house where Marie and some village women sat talking. I kept hearing in my ears: "We're going to present *our* gun.... our gun...." Almost as if it were a broken record stuck on the plural possessive pronoun it kept repeating in my ears, "*ngale jangan.... ngale jangan....*" Before I reached the house I had thought of half a dozen very good reasons why I should say no. However I got the gun and some shells and started back to the clubhouse. As I re-entered the room I caught again the sense of the world of Obam Nna. If I were to be Obam Nna, I should have to cease to be William Reyburn. In order to be Obam Nna, I had to crucify William Reyburn every day. In the world of Obam Nna I no longer owned a gun as in the world of William Reyburn. I handed the gun to the chief and, although he didn't know it, along with it went the surrender of a very stingy idea of private ownership.

The material by William D. Reyburn in this Unit is from the article "Identification in the Missionary Task" from *Readings in Missionary Anthropology* (William Carey Library 1978).

LIMITS OF IDENTIFICATION

William D. Reyburn

Perhaps the most outstanding example in which I was reminded of the limitations of identification occurred while we were living in a mud-and-thatch hut near Tabacundo, Ecuador. We had moved into a small scattered farming settlement near the Pisque River about a kilometre from the United Andean Mission for whom we were making a study. My wife and I had agreed that if we were to accomplish anything at the U.A.M. we would have to settle among the people and somehow get them to accept us or reject us. We were accepted eventually but always with reservations. We wore nothing but Indian clothes and ate nothing but Indian food. We had no furniture except a bed made of century plant stalks covered with a woven mat exactly as in all the Indian houses. In fact, because we had no agricultural equipment, weaving loom or granary, our one-room house was by far the most empty in the vicinity. In spite of this material reduction to the zero point, the men addressed me as *patroncito*. When I objected that I was not a *patron* because I owned no land, they reminded me that I wore leather shoes. I quickly exchanged these for a pair of locally made *alpargatas* which have a hemp fibre sole and a woven cotton upper. After a time had passed I noticed that merely changing my footwear had not

in the least gotten rid of the appellation *patroncito*. When I asked again the men replied that I associated with the Spanish townspeople from Tabacundo. In so doing I was obviously identifying myself with the *patron* class. I made every effort for a period to avoid the townspeople, but the term *patroncito* seemed to be as permanently fixed as it was the day we moved into the community.

The men had been required by the local commissioner to repair an impassable road connecting the community and Tabacundo. I joined in this work with the Indians until it was completed two months later. My hands had become hard and calloused. One day I proudly showed my calloused hands to a group of men while they were finishing the last of a jar of fermented *chica*. "Now, you can't say I don't work with you. Why do you still call me *patroncito*?" This time the truth was near the surface, forced there by uninhibited alcoholic replies. Vicento Cuzco, a leader in the group, stepped up and put his arm around my shoulder and whispered to me. "We call you *patroncito* because you weren't born of an Indian mother." I needed no further explanation.

There are two major factors in building relationships with people of other cultures. The first relates to our attitudes. We have already seen the importance of identification with people who are different from us. This is based on attitudes such as love, respect, acceptance and trust. The second factor is equally important, though often overlooked. One of the biggest problems in another culture is that at first we simply do not understand the way things are done. We do not know how to do even simple things, which we take for granted in our own culture – how to go shopping, order food in a restaurant, use public

transport, make conversation with different types of people, or know when humour is appropriate. We lack social skills and have to learn them all over again in the new culture.

It is important to be aware of both factors as we try to build relationships. We shall look at them more closely in Units 5 and 6. You can study these two Units in whichever order you like. Remember that we need both the right attitudes and appropriate social skills. Otherwise we shall always feel ourselves on the outside.

ACCEPTANCE AND TRUST

CONTENTS

PURPOSE

This Unit helps you explore some of the personal issues involved in gaining the acceptance and trust of people in another culture.

ACCEPTING OURSELVES

If we have a poor self-image we shall be too concerned about our being accepted by others to be able to think about how we accept them.

The basis of good relationships with others is the acceptance of them as individuals and their way of life as a valid one. We may not even be able to begin to do this unless we have already accepted ourselves.

The Problem of Prestige

Most of us feel a sense of self-worth when prestige is ascribed to us because of our social position or what we think we've achieved through our accomplishments. But in some cultures prestige is ascribed because of the formal credentials of birth and rank. In others it is won by personal achievement.

The Prestige of Social Position

Individuals whose life-style reflects prestige ascribed because of social position will find servanthood uncomfortable. When I was teaching in Jamaica we expected the girls to keep their surroundings tidy. One day a teacher asked two sisters to pick up paper they had strewn on the floor. A few days later their irate mother confronted the Headmistress saying, "My girls do not pick up litter from the floor".

If we are concerned about social prestige we will probably opt for living in a socially acceptable suburb in the place to which we go.

- The rich young ruler (Luke 19) was concerned to be acceptable by adhering to the commandments, but he could not bear to give up the prestige his riches gave him.

- By contrast, Martha (Luke 10) though critical of her sister Mary, was willing to undertake the humble job in the kitchen for the service of Christ. (Perhaps she was unconsciously looking for recognition as well?)

> **Relying on personal prestige, in whatever way, is in opposition to the career of servanthood which God has for all believers.**

The Prestige of Achievement

Romans 3.10-18 tells us that none of us deserves prestige. Our self-worth in human terms is nil. All of us find it hard to accept this, especially in cultures where prestige based on personal achievement is important.

But in spite of our inherent worthlessness and empty self-righteousness God finds worth in us, not a self-worth gained by human effort but a worth based on the grace and love He demonstrated to us in His son Jesus (Romans 3.21-24). Jesus "....did not come to be served but to serve, and to give his life as a ransom for many" (Mark 10.45).

We have to recognise that our self-worth comes from who we are in Jesus, not what we are in ourselves.

And this implies living a life of servanthood.

Servanthood also implies accepting God's shaping of our personal life as good. If we are not able to do this in our native culture we will never be able to accept it when we move to another. Nor will we be able to accept worth in the life of others who are culturally different from us. So we need to accept without reserve God's work in our lives as good.

However, all this does not mean that we must blot out our individual personality and personal cultural history. Jesus is fully God and fully Man. He grew up in actions and ways like a first century Jew but he did not forget that his home was in heaven and his destiny was to be the Messiah, not just for those of his own race but for the whole world.

Here are some questions for personal reflection.

Does servanthood require us to be subject to the rulers and authorities and social customs of the society in which God has placed us — even when this is a culture where prestige is ascribed by social position?

Self Acceptance

■ Do I like myself? Why? Why not?

■ Can I accept myself — and not like myself?

■ Why is acceptance of self the beginning point of change?

■ Why must I accept myself before I can accept others?

■ As a Christian, what basis do I have for self-acceptance?

■ What do Christians who reject themselves (the creatures) infer about God (the one who created them) through their self-rejection?

■ What steps do I need to take to accept myself more fully?

Self-acceptance is not self-approval — it is self-acknowledgement.

ACCEPTING OTHERS

ACCEPTING THE CONTEXT

There are hundreds of cultural contexts in the world and they are all valid and useful to the people who share them. Our challenge is to accept the differences in others and even to be multi-cultural – that is to be able to work from our own culture into the culture of others and to live in their way.

This is not a simple task. Most of our lives we have lived in our native culture. We have never questioned this context but simply assumed it is the correct one.

Before we begin to learn to live in a different culture we must learn to accept the change of context. We must believe that this is valid and potentially good and recognise that our understanding of our own culture is inadequate. We have to begin to learn in the new context as children, yet with the speed and wisdom of an adult.

To attempt to belong to a group whose standards and behaviour conflict with our own does lead to cultural stress. But if we are to make real relationships with people of another culture we must accept their culture as just as valid a way of life as our own, whatever the inherent imperfections of both may be.

This does not demand or imply loss of moral integrity. The key to growth and maturity in cross-cultural ministry is complete submission and dependence - not on the other culture, but on God.

TRUSTING THE PEOPLE

Our primary aim in forming relationships with those of another culture must be to develop mutual respect based on trust. We should ask ourselves, "Is what I am doing, thinking or saying building trust or undermining it?" We must consistently check up on ourselves in regard to our attitudes and actions towards others.

For example, if we think black or darker skinned people are inferior to ourselves it will inevitably come over in the way we treat and speak to them. On the other hand, if we feel resentful towards white people, or people of another country which fought with our country, it will also show itself.

We must particularly learn how other people view time, space and causation, especially of the origins of the earth and what causes disease or death. We need to "get inside" people's heads to see how they perceive the world.

We can help ourselves to do this by getting to know their mythology. This will tell us a lot about their worldview (see Unit 1). Learning to understand their use of symbols will also help us to understand their basic values. An image of Buddha or a cross on the wall of a home will at once tell us where the religious allegiance of the family lies.

Though learning about another culture is not a guarantee of our acceptance into it, it does help us with the process of identification.

Accepting People who are Different

Identify some behaviour that is common among non-Christians of your culture but is inappropriate for you.

- What do I typically do when this behaviour is done in my presence?

- Does my behaviour increase or decrease that person's trust relationship with me? Why?

- Is there some way to accept such a person at such a moment without losing my witness?

- What did I assume was involved in "losing my witness" in the last question?

- How does acceptance and trust relate to my witness?

- In what ways does Jesus' behaviour indicate acceptance (in what circumstances)?

- In what ways does Jesus' behaviour indicate rejection (in what circumstances)?

INTERVIEWS

As you continue your interviews, you can reflect on this matter of building trust and acceptance in relationships. Look particularly at the reflection material for Sessions 2 and 3.

GOOD RELATIONSHIPS

Superficial friendships with others will help us to learn something about their culture but unless we form real friendships with them we shall remain an outsider in their culture. For this to take place there must be acceptance of each other at a deep level. This does not happen automatically. It involves effort, determination and skill. It demands a desire to love, accompanied by the consistent development and application of human relationship skills.

Some barriers that hinder good interpersonal relationships:

It would be incorrect to assume that all of these are deliberate attempts to hinder cross-cultural relations. Some are indeed sinful and avoidable, others may be ingrained attitudes, perhaps copied from parental examples. But whatever their origin they need to be acknowledged and brought to the Lord so that He can deal with them and help us to replace them with positive and helpful attitudes.

Some personal traits to watch out for:

A patronising manner

We must be careful not to give the impression that we are doing others a favour in making friends with them. They do not want us to do things for but with them. They want to be accepted as equals. We have to learn from them, listen to their needs and beware of doing all the talking.

Pride

To start with we automatically think our ways are best. We must be willing to admit some deficiencies in our way of life and receive criticism graciously. At the same time we must genuinely appreciate and respect the accomplishments and culture of our friend. Nothing creates more resentment than a superior attitude (often unconscious).

Superficiality

We must be prepared to spend time with friends, revealing in a personal way that we have their interests at heart. It is much better to see a few people frequently and get to know them well rather than knowing ten or twenty people casually and superficially.

Lack of understanding

It is most important that we take trouble to get to know our host culture and avoid asking foolish questions or thinking thoughts that reveal assumptions of backwardness and inferiority. We must also realise that this or that is not the right or wrong way but simply different.

As Christians we should examine our lives and see whether any of these inappropriate attitudes exist and confess them if they do. We can thank God for our own culture and the privilege we have because we come from it. We can also thank God for other's cultures. We don't have a choice as to where we are born or what race we are, so to be proud about this or prejudiced towards others because of what God has made them can only be termed a sin.

We will only form close relationships with the people of another culture if we learn to trust each other. Mutual respect will build up gradually as we grow in love and appreciation of one another. This takes time. Flexibility and adaptability are essential. There are barriers to be overcome – the obvious differences such as climate, food, modes of transport, people's appearance and colour. These all challenge our capacity to adapt. Along with these is the fact that we lack the social skills of the local culture, as we have already noted. If we are not observant and sensitive we can sow seeds of misunderstanding, friction and hostility which will take a very long time to eradicate.

LIVING WITH A LOCAL FAMILY

The first few weeks in a new culture are critical in determining the ease with which a person will adapt to it. We can prepare ourselves as best we know beforehand, but it is the critical emotional progress in the early days which will indelibly stamp our responses to our new neighbours and work colleagues. Our senses are bombarded by a multitude of new sensations, sights, sounds and smells. At this point it is all exciting and interest is at its peak.

On arrival we are in a state of unique readiness, both physically and emotionally, to learn to belong in a new environment.

We must see the importance of establishing a sense of bonding with local people as crucial and try to avoid becoming intimate with others of our own culture rather than the people of the new society. This happens in subtle ways, especially when the expatriates, out of goodwill for the newcomer, are friendly and warmly hospitable. We need to be tactful about accepting such invitations in preference to those of local people.

If you can arrange to live with a local family at an early stage, this has many advantages. It helps you to learn how insiders organise their life – how they get their food and do their shopping, how they get around by public transport, how they feel about the way outsiders live.

Experiencing an alternative lifestyle can help a person evaluate the question of adopting it for oneself and one's own family. Otherwise you may automatically continue in your own familiar way. Once this has been done it is very difficult to change. Of course, being so enveloped in the local culture at such an early stage of one's experience in it can be stressful. It is not easy to live with a family with very different customs from one's own, and to make friends with numerous strangers. (But neither is it easy to continue as a stranger without knowing the local cultural views, and leading a foreign lifestyle with all of the time, effort and orientation that this involves). However, because we are experiencing close relationships we are able to derive support from these local friendships and this gives us a sense of feeling at home.

As we have learned to accept ourselves and learned to accept friends in our new culture as of equal worth in God's sight, we will form the bonding that will enable us to build up mutual trust. Then we will be able to share the gospel of Christ in a more meaningful way than we otherwise could.

Unit **6**

SOCIAL
SKILLS

CONTENTS

PURPOSE

This Unit will help you to identify the kinds of social skills you will
need to learn in a new culture.

A QUESTION OF SKILLS

It is true that we may need to change our attitudes and relate to people with acceptance and trust, as we have discussed in Unit 5. But if we think only about our attitudes there is a danger of becoming introspective or even depressed, thinking that there is something wrong with us because of our failure to "adjust". It is equally important for us to learn the social skills of the new culture.

The quotations on this page are from *Cultures in Contact*, Stephen Bochner (ed.), Pergamon Press 1982, page 164.

We feel strange because we are not used to the way things are done. We need to learn how to do them in an appropriate way – shopping, meeting people, doing business, relaxing, negotiating traffic, getting repairs done, going to the bank.

These are all skills. We take them for granted in our own culture, because we have absorbed them unconsciously. We have to learn them again, consciously, in our new culture.

There are great advantages in understanding cultural adaptation in this way.

"The major task facing a sojourner is not to adjust to a new culture, but to learn its salient characteristics. In particular, if the sojourner is to work effectively in the new setting, and lead a relatively stress-free and fulfilling life, the person must acquire the social skills of the host culture, especially knowledge necessary to negotiate everyday social encounters with members of the receiving society."

This has two major consequences:

- **"Failures and problems experienced by the sojourner need not be regarded as symptoms of some underlying pathology, but rather due to a lack of the necessary cultural skills and knowledge… remedial action involves imparting appropriate knowledge and skills…"**

- **"'Adjusting' a person to a culture has connotations of cultural chauvinism, implying that the newcomer should abandon the culture of origin in favour of embracing the values and customs of the host society. On the other hand, learning a second culture has no such ethnocentric overtones. There are many examples in life when it becomes necessary to learn a practice even if one does not approve of it, and then abandon the custom when circumstances have changed."**

So our task, when we arrive in a new culture, is to learn. For this we need to be observant and curious – to see *what* people do and *why*.

To Copy?

As we try to learn the local customs it is important to realise that a particular social skill is not intrinsically desirable or advisable in itself. It must be judged in relation to the cultural circumstances which make a particular behaviour appropriate or inappropriate. A casual, superficial copying may do more harm than good if we do not relate whatever we see and hear to the context in which we find ourselves. We have all heard stories of unsuspecting visitors being taught words and phrases, perhaps by children, which they repeated proudly to their adult friends. When their friends looked shocked, or perhaps laughed, they found out they had been taught some very unrepeatable swearwords...

To Conform?

In some cases we will realise that it is essential for us to conform to the local rules, for example, in the matter of eating and drinking. In other cases we may feel we can adhere to our native habits. The answers to how we should behave are not always black and white nor are the reasons why local people do things a certain way necessarily easy to understand. We should learn to recognise what the local rules are, try to understand them and never simply condemn them.

Being Patient

We must try not to be offended by ways that are different from ours and remember to be patient. Cross-cultural relationships are like relating to a new person. We must seek to understand them and their situation, listen and watch. We should not be concerned with the impression we are making on them. If we do this we shall be under a sense of strain which may come across in a way we do not intend. Others may think we are not genuine or feel superior or lacking in real love.

It is important that we don't just observe but consciously think through what we see and hear and consider how we can adapt to the local customs and ideas.

We are not alone

Learning to live in another culture is hard work. We should never give up aiming to become incarnate in the culture we have entered. We are not alone. Jesus Christ went the same way and could understand, sympathise and enable us to go beyond what we are naturally capable of.

> *"Americans will find that they have to stand much closer to an Arab during interaction in the Middle East than they would with fellow-Americans at home. Japanese must learn to have more eye-contact with westerners during conversation than is customary in their own culture. Australians in Great Britain of necessity have to learn to drink warm beer, a habit they discard as soon as they depart."*
> *(Furnham and Bochner)*

What follows is a survey of some of the main areas in which we need to observe and learn. It is general, of course, and the examples given are just illustrations. You will have to find the specific details for each culture when you encounter it. And remember that cultures are changing all the time. New ways of doing things are constantly emerging and there can be great variations between urban and rural situations in the same culture.

There are innumerable customs and different ways of doing things in different cultures. The best way to handle situations we are uncertain about is to ask a local person whom we know well and can trust for advice.

INTERVIEWS

You will use this material in Session 3 of your interviews (see the guidelines).

PRACTICAL SURVIVAL

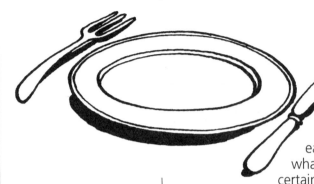

Food

The social context, especially over a meal, is the best place to build relationships with people of another culture. At the same time, you need to be aware that there are strict rules concerning eating and drinking in most cultures. They include what may or may not be eaten or drunk, especially certain kinds of meat (pork, beef) and alcohol. There may be actual laws forbidding certain things, like consuming alcohol in certain Arab countries. There are also written rules about how eating is performed (knife and fork, chopsticks, right hand), and extensive rules about table manners (when to start eating, how much to leave on your plate, how to obtain or refuse second helpings). In some cultures women eat separately from men.

In many cultures people express their appreciation of visits by offering food or drink and may be highly offended if this is refused. This may be especially important on the first visit to a person's home. We should usually eat whatever is offered, even if we dislike it. It may be that sometimes the standard of hygiene is not what we are accustomed to, but I believe that in a situation where the refusal of food would cause offence we can trust the Lord with the problem of possible after-effects.

In some cultures it is very rude to say yes to an invitation the first time it is given. To do so is thought to be greedy. To ask only once is thought to be selfish and to indicate that you do not really mean it. The prospective host must ask a person several times before the person will feel it correct to accept the invitation.

Some cultures have well defined rules about seating guests, especially on formal occasions. There may also be rules about whom to talk to – the person on the right or the left or opposite.

Time

The concept of "being late" varies greatly in different cultures. In some you may be five minutes late for an appointment, but not fifteen and certainly not thirty. In others it is normal. To arrive late may be seen as a sign of importance. In some cultures you may arrive five to fifteen minutes late for an invitation to dinner. In others someone might arrive two hours late, three hours late – or not at all, because they only accepted the invitation to prevent the host losing face.

In some cultures you may have to wait several days for your turn at a government office. There may be professional "waiters" to do this for you.

POLITENESS

Some countries approve of a person who makes a request politely but directly. Others regard such openness as a form of weakness or treachery. They think you shouldn't allow the outside world to penetrate your thoughts.

In some cultures it is thought polite to exaggerate about your abilities and achievements, in others to be excessively modest. Sometimes people ask questions rather than giving orders when making requests, so that "Would you like to do so and so?" implies that you should obey. A special form of words may be used for special situations such as disagreeing in committee meetings or introducing people to each other. The intensity with which speech is uttered also varies. Some speak loudly and others may interpret this as shouting or label them "brash".

GIFTS

In all cultures it is necessary to present relatives, friends and work colleagues with gifts on certain occasions. But rules vary greatly. Some spend a great deal on gifts which must be bought from standard gift shops so that their value can be ascertained and a gift of the same value returned. In other cultures wedding gifts are given to the bride and bridegroom's parents and other relatives rather than to the couple being married. On the birth of a baby certain relatives have to give a certain number of gifts to the new-born according to their relationship to the baby. In some cultures it is rude to open gifts in the presence of the giver. In others the reverse is the case.

CUES OF INTENTION

In every culture certain actions indicate what people intend to do. Muslims, Hindus and Sikhs remove their shoes as they enter a place of worship. If they invite a priest to say prayers in their home they spread a white sheet over the floor of the room where this is to take place, remove their shoes when they enter and sit around the edges of the room. Some Pacific Islanders chew betel-nut before initiating a conversation. In Britain we offer people a cup of tea or coffee if we mean them to stay with us awhile.

BRIBERY

In many places it is normal to pay a commission to civil servants, salesmen or professional people who have performed a service, although they are already receiving a salary. This is regarded as perfectly normal while in other cultures it is unethical and termed bribery. In many cases it is actually illegal.

BUYING AND SELLING

There are different sets of rules for this in different cultures – barter, bargaining, fixed price and so on. In cultures where bargaining is used it is normal to establish a relationship first, perhaps while drinking tea. Then there are conventions about how the bargaining should proceed.

POSTURE

In some cultures where furniture is uncommon various postures are customary – squatting, kneeling or leaning on a spear.

GESTURES

These vary in different cultures. Some people shake hands or embrace when greeting each other. Others bow to one another or use different hand gestures. In Britain people shake their head to indicate disagreement but in Southern Italy it is indicated by a head toss. A raised thumb is a sign of approval in Britain; in Greece it is an insult.

Does one give to beggars in countries where begging is a profession? What should one do about accepting gifts from people who are very poor?

GETTING CLOSER

DISTANCE

Cultural misunderstandings often arise out of actions done unconsciously. This is illustrated in the way people use physical space when they stand talking to each other. Some cultures stand at a distance of about a metre and a half when discussing general matters. When they want to discuss a more personal matter they will approach within a metre and lower their voices. Others stand much closer and also face each other more directly.

Misunderstandings arise when people from different cultures meet. One may move within a metre in order to converse. The other, feeling a bit uneasy at this distance, may move a step back. The first one, feeling that he is having to talk "across the room", steps within his range again. As the conversation progresses (or breaks down) the one may get the impression that the other is cold and distant or too familiar. In many cultures the rules break down when people crowd together in lifts and buses, at football matches and parties.

GAZE

Some countries have special rules about gaze, such as that you should not look at certain parts of the body. Some have a high level of gaze and may label Europeans whose gaze is low as aloof, cold and unfriendly. A person accustomed to a high gaze may interpret a low gaze as impolite, a sign of not paying attention or being dishonest. A person accustomed to a low one may regard a high gaze as disrespectful, threatening or insulting.

Eye contact also differs in different cultures. In some cultures it is usual to look at the person to whom you are speaking but in others people drop their gaze. A woman in particular should drop her gaze if talking to a man. On the other hand it is rude to stare in some cultures, but in others, especially in the villages, people stare openly and will often crowd round your door to see what you are doing, especially if you are new to them.

TOUCHING

In some cultures touch is common, in others a brief handshake is all that is expected. In some cultures it is only used under restricted conditions such as with a family. In some cultures a woman does not touch her husband in public though two men may embrace openly in the street.

FACIAL EXPRESSIONS

These may indicate attitudes, express emotions, elaborate speech and provide feedback to the listener. They may indicate when it is someone's turn to speak or listen, or when it is appropriate to interrupt. In different cultures they differ widely. In some, negative facial expression is forbidden, hence the impression that they are "inscrutable" people. In others, people may smile and laugh when very angry.

FACE SAVING

In many Eastern cultures maintaining face is of great importance. In South Asia maintaining "izzat" or family honour is the first duty of its members. Special skills are required to make sure that others do not lose face. In negotiations it may be necessary to make token concessions before the other side can give way. Great care must be taken at meetings over disagreeing or criticising people.

ASSERTIVENESS

Western culture tends to value assertiveness. But in some cultures assertiveness is not valued and submission or the maintenance of pleasant social relations are valued more. In the East disagreements are avoided or at least confined to members of the same family or group.

AGGRESSION

Different cultures vary in how they express or react to aggression. In some it is correct to say nothing and submit to whatever insult or unfairness is being perpetrated. In others it is commendable to stand up for your rights.

HUMOUR

This differs widely in different cultures. When we come into a new one we should at first be restrained in our humorous remarks and watch and listen until we know what is thought amusing in the local culture. The favourite British prank of "leg pulling" can in some other cultures upset people deeply – they do not see it as funny but as a personal insult. Ethnic jokes and anecdotes such as the parsimony of the Scots reinforce stereotypes and should always be avoided. As should such phrases as "Dutch treat", "Chinese puzzle", or "take French leave". They are usually incomprehensible and can also cause offence.

COMPLAINTS

It is not correct in all cultures to address complaints directly to the person you consider responsible. Some cultures think it cowardly not to do this, but in others it is more direct to use a go-between to settle misunderstandings.

TABOOS

These occur in every culture. For example, in some cultures sex should never be brought into the conversation. In others, death or religion are avoided as topics. Muslims are offended by those who eat pork; other cultures view dogs with horror. Sitting so that the soles of your feet face the other person is offensive in some cultures or sitting so that your feet point at someone. It is particularly important to know whether men and women mix freely or whether they only associate in public with the same sex.

You can use the information in this Unit as a discussion starter with friends from other cultures. You can ask them how they do things in their culture and share how you do them. They may be wanting to learn social skills from your culture as well.

THE INNER WORLD

FAMILY RELATIONSHIPS

In many countries the family is more important than it is in the West. A wide range of relatives are actively involved in family life and decisions. They have a sense of closeness and make considerable demands on each other. They help each other pay for education, get jobs, and solve problems when in trouble. Marriage is a contract arranged between families rather than just the two individuals concerned. Dowries or bride prices are often paid. In some societies polygamy is accepted. Older people are usually highly respected. Large financial contributions are made to the family by younger working members who have left home.

Sex roles vary. In Arab societies women do not work but spend most of their time at home. In other countries like China they do nearly the same job as men. In Indian villages women do a major part of the work in the fields. Cultures vary from complete promiscuity before marriage to a complete ban on sex outside marriage. Business men visiting some foreign countries may be offered girls as part of hospitality but in others there are the strictest of taboos on sex outside marriage. West Europeans mix work and family life and receive visitors in the home. Japanese and Arabs do not.

GROUPS

In some countries, the individual is subordinate to the group and a high degree of conformity is expected. In Japan group decisions are generally carried by general acquiescence to the will of the group, without voting. In some countries there is great stress on cooperation rather than competition in groups, for example in Israeli Kibbutzim and Mexican villages. In India where the caste system (though outlawed by government) is still widespread especially in villages, particular castes will live in the same part of the village, have their own well and never eat or have social relations with anyone from a different caste.

In Africa work groups are usually made up from members of the same tribe. To appoint a leader from another tribe would be disastrous. In some cultures there are greater social distinctions between ranks and more deference and obedience to people in high positions. Subordinates do not speak freely in front of more senior people, and face to face discussion is less common.

Personal ownership is viewed differently in different cultures. Some lay great stress on this while in other cultures it doesn't exist; everything someone has is expected to be available to other members of the group if they need it. (Remember the story about the gun in Unit 4).

HELPING RELATIVES

In many countries people are expected to help their relatives and this is the equivalent of social welfare. Sometimes relatives have contributed to an individual's education; when the relative gets a good job they expect something in return. But there are usually local rules which limit the form such favours may take.

MOURNING

Funeral ceremonies vary widely in different cultures and visitors who attend should be careful to do as the local people do. In many cultures there are elaborate rules about mourning as there used to be in Britain before the Second World War. The Jews used to tear their clothes as a symbol of the inner tearing they felt in parting with a loved one. British people try to be "brave" and hide the way they feel about losing a loved one. In India if someone does so they are thought not to care. Not only the relatives but all who visit the bereaved family are expected to weep openly. In some villages there are women who are expected to attend a funeral for the specific job of wailing profusely. Anyone who knew the deceased even slightly, is expected to attend the funeral.

IDEAS

Certain aspects of life within another culture can be incomprehensible without an understanding of the underlying ideas. Some of them are carried by language, so knowing the language deepens your understanding of a culture. Attitudes to business practices are greatly affected by ideology. Muslims used to regard paying interest as sinful. The Protestant work ethic is compatible with capitalism.

Muslims also have strict rules based on religious ideas, such as fasting during Ramadan, saying prayers five times a day, and giving one-fortieth of their money to the poor.

There are different rules for different occasions. The British go on picnics. Chinese families go to pay respect to their ancestors. There are special services connected with engagement, marriage, childbirth, funerals, which reflect the ideas behind them.

ACHIEVEMENT

Though there are wide variations within a culture, in some circles individuals work hard and take risks to earn money, improve their status and build up the enterprise in which they work. In others people expect to be rewarded on the basis of the social position of their family or tribe rather than because of their own effort. In orthodox Hinduism the caste into which someone is born decrees the work they do, which can limit the potential for individual achievement.

Read the chapter on "Worldview Change" (chapter 8 in the 1990 edition, chapter 9 in the 2001 edition). This highlights the fact that cultures change in various ways. They are never static – except for very traditional ones, which are increasingly rare.

Old and New

In many cultures there are two sets of rules and ideas corresponding to traditional and modern attitudes. These centre round independence from parental authority, concern to conform to the peer group, openness to new experiences, the role of women. Often young people adopt some form of compromise, finding themselves caught between the old and the new. Should a visitor identify with and encourage the old or the new? This is something we need to think through.

Material on this page is by Ruth Bachelor.

HOW TO DISCOVER THE STRUCTURES OF A COMMUNITY

These suggestions are to help you make friends and not merely to make you knowledgeable. Be sensitive in asking the questions. But if you can find the answers to most of these questions you will have learned a great deal about the culture in which you find yourself. However, note that the questions are very much geared to a rural situation and would need adaptation to an urban setting.

Community leaders

■ Who makes the community decisions? Who exercises the authority of the government? (Make sure you show the expected courtesies.)

The household tasks

■ Note the cooking equipment used. How is food prepared before cooking? What fuel is used? How is it obtained? Watch the cooking process. Copy and eat! What combinations of food are eaten? Is it a mixed diet: cereals, legumes, roots? Is animal protein used? When? What variations in diet occur at different times? Does the whole family eat the same? What fruits are available, and when? What fat is use, and how? How is food stored? What problems arise? How are perishable foods preserved? Does food get short at times? When?

■ What is the source of water? How often is this collected? From how far? Is it available all the year round? What alternative sources are there? (Visit the water source.) What happens to human and animal faeces?

■ What home accidents occur? How are they treated? With what success? Is lighting used? Heating? What things must the family buy or pay for in cash? How do they find the money? How is it kept safe?

Crafts and skills

■ What crafts do the women do? Which are especially for men? If you are a woman, learn to spin and weave from a local housewife, or try to winnow or make pots. If you are a man, ask to be taught to thatch or make a mat, or join a hunting or canoeing expedition. Study forest work, trap-making, fishing methods, blacksmithing and local building. Try several different skills. Visit the makers of tools and farming equipment.

Parents and children

■ How do men spend the day? Does this vary with the season? What do they enjoy most? What do men chat about informally? How do women spend the different hours of the day? What does she enjoy most; and chat about informally? How do

they show their concern and support for those in trouble?

■ What are the first solids offered to babies? At what age are they weaned? What problems arise? Who disciplines the children: the toddler? The under six-year-old? The six to twelve-year-old? The teenager? How do children learn, and from whom? Note their games and manual skills.

■ What kind of behaviour do parents particularly encourage, or discourage, What is courteous behaviour? What is discourteous? How does this vary towards elders, contemporaries and juniors? What must you personally learn from this?

Celebrations

■ What celebrations are held during the year? What ceremonies take place? (Before planting, at ripening of the first crop, harvest, birth, marriage, death, etc.)

The extended family

■ Who influences family decisions about emergencies, schooling, marriage, making changes, sickness and treatment, birth practices, etc.? To whom do young husbands, or young wives, go for advice? What are the privileges and responsibilities of belonging to the extended family?

Making close friends

■ Most likely, you will relate best to the young, lively and articulate, and this is natural. However, in many societies their opinions will not be respected as much as those of older people. If you do not make your friendships exclusively with one age group or one section of a community, then you will enjoy the give and take of discussion, reasoning and support from many different perspectives.

■ We found that by inviting people to our home in groups rather than as individuals they were less shy. In some cases, we played ridiculous games together; in others, we had Bible discussions. Both helped to break down barriers, and I am sure we learnt as much as any of our visitors, most of whom came regularly and grew to be our close advisers.

OTHER FAITHS

CONTENTS

PURPOSE

The Unit will help you in the practical issues of how to relate positively to people of other faith communities.

TALKING ABOUT RELIGION

Many people who claim to be "searching" for a new faith may not know the official teachings of their own religion.

We may find people of other cultures opening up conversations about religious matters and questioning us about our faith, long before we would expect them to. In many cultures religion is talked about much more freely than in countries like Britain.

We should beware of thinking that this means they intend to adopt our faith for themselves. It may be nothing more than cultural curiosity. In many countries religion and culture are inseparable.

Western and Christian

As our world shrinks and information about other countries becomes available everywhere, we may find that people of other faiths have a low view of Christianity. They compare the standards of morality in their own religion with what they see of Western culture in the media,

assuming this is Christian. If they tell us that they feel this way, we can use this as an opportunity to explain that "Western" and "Christian" behaviour are not one and the same thing, and perhaps suggest that they read the New Testament to see for themselves the standards that Jesus set.

It is not only Christians who go to other cultures and share their faith. Many belonging to sects of Christianity and of other religions are very zealous evangelists. If they are from the West people may assume that they are all teaching Christianity. They may also never have had access to documents containing the essential doctrines of Christianity. It is up to us to show what true Christianity is.

Stress the Similarities

It is better not to start by emphasising ways in which we differ. The best means of building a friendly atmosphere is to talk first about beliefs we have in common. This does not mean that we should not be aware of differences in their faith, for example different ideas about sin and its remedy. Later when we have built up a friendship we can focus on these areas.

We may notice potential areas of misunderstanding, such as the Incarnation for Hindus, Buddhists and Sikhs. They may confuse this with reincarnation. Other areas may be eternal life, meditation, sin, or the Trinity.

We will find that no two people view their religion in exactly the same way. We should discover how they view and experience their faith before attempting to point out similarities and differences between their beliefs and ours.

Eye Openers

From the evidence of Scripture and the history of Christianity it is apparent that God does not leave cultures without their own witness to Him. By carefully examining the religious teaching and traditions of a culture we may find analogies to serve as vessels for the gospel message. These serve as "eye openers" in terms of people's understanding of our message.

Attitudes

The first thing we must examine before we start sharing our faith with people of another faith, is our attitude towards them. The key word is "servant". We must be prepared to act as Christ's servants and also the servants of those whose culture we have entered (1 Corinthians 9.19).

This may mean giving up some of our freedoms which may hinder the gospel. In rural India a woman should always have her head covered in public. Not to do so indicates that she has lower moral standards, which of course reflects on the Christian message she is trying to proclaim.

We will need to enter the other person's world in order to win their friendship and trust. It is in the context of someone's worldview that they will decide on and evaluate our message. We must accept their world view as valid in their context and never ridicule it. The good aspects of culture can be used as a bridge for the gospel and as a launch point for its contextualisation. Contextualisation is undertaken through defining, selecting, adapting and applying the message. As we do this we also learn how to deliver the message in the appropriate style.

Only as we become trustworthy friends of others, will we be able to come to the point of sharing the gospel. We may adapt to their style of living and eating, and this is helpful, but it will mean nothing unless they know that we love them for themselves.

We will have to spend time with them revealing in a personal way that we have their interests at heart. It is better to get to know one or two people well than ten or twenty people superficially. From the days of the Exodus the rule to "love your neighbour as yourself" was part of Jewish law. When a lawyer asked Jesus, "What must I do to receive eternal life?" (Luke 10.25) Jesus answered that the two greatest commandments were to love God and love one's neighbour as oneself. When the lawyer asked "Who is my neighbour?" Jesus told the parable of the good Samaritan in reply.

Alongside love must go our prayers for those friends with whom we hope to share the good news of Jesus. Without that, little will be accomplished.

"Go, then to all peoples everywhere and make them my disciples" (Matthew 28.19). Scripture makes it plain that we are to share our faith cross-culturally. Acts contains a number of stories of Peter, Paul and other Jews sharing the Gospel with the Gentiles. Our heavenly Father is a missionary God with a world-wide vision.

SHARING ...

Motives

The first reaction when we show kindness to a person of another faith may be "What is their motive?" If they know we are Christians they may suspect we want to convert them. So it is most important that their confidence should be established on a friendship basis and any discussion of religious subjects should be natural and not forced. If our approach is tactful and there is a reality in our friendship, we may soon find an opportunity to share our faith. When they recognise that our friendship does not depend on their acceptance of Christianity, they will be much more relaxed and free to consider objectively what we have to say.

Respect

We should never imply that we are doing people a favour by offering them the benefits of our faith, or appear to write off their faith because we cannot agree with certain parts of it. They value the teaching of their own heritage, especially its morals. Rather than tell them what is wrong with their faith we should emphasise the positive help we find in Christianity. This does not mean papering over problems or pretending there are no differences between religions, but approaching differences in a way that will be perceived as loving.

Arguments

It is generally unwise to get involved in philosophical discussions and arguments. Many religions contain a lot of philosophical teaching, more so than in Christianity, and well taught followers often enjoy abstract discussion. But this often leads nowhere as far as witnessing for Christ is concerned. Getting involved in heated arguments creates bad feeling all round. Quietly telling how Jesus has worked in our life is far more effective.

Meeting Needs

Most people have a variety of physical as well as spiritual needs. If we do nothing to help them with these they are unlikely to listen when we try to press the claims of Christ. They will feel we don't care about them as individuals but only as potential converts. Jesus always ministered to people's immediate needs. He fed the five thousand, healed Peter's mother-in-law and came to his disciples in a storm. Caring can open the way to a person's heart but must be genuine. At its deepest level it does mean caring that a person should find eternal life in the Lord Jesus Christ. But this usually takes a lot of time and patience and much genuine caring for caring's sake.

Meanwhile we can look for internal needs and questions that can be answered in Christ, such as the meaning of death, the purpose of life, is there a God who cares for me? And be sensitive to crisis opportunities for sharing Jesus' love in every way we can.

Don't be Pushy!

We should never push our beliefs at people. Anyone will resent an approach that implies we are not interested in them as individuals but only in ourselves and in changing them. When we build a genuine relationship they will be interested to hear how we came to know God and have peace with him, to be forgiven, and have assurance of heaven.

We must never imply that we are superior because of our colour, background or education, or even because we are Christians.

Clash of Worlds

Read the chapters on New Religious Movements (chapters 9 and 10 in the 1990 edition, chapters 10 and 11 in the 2001 edition). These describe one way in which cultures change. Have you come across any similar examples of new movements, which mix elements from older religions and cultural patterns? What do they tell us about what people are looking for?

You may like to read again chapter 14, which you read earlier. It should be helpful as you think of relating to a person of a different faith.

... AND CARING

Conversion – A Betrayal?

We must realise that in many cultures, family, community and religious faith are closely bound up together. A commitment to Christ may be seen as a betrayal of all these. The person converting from another faith will face opposition from their family and religious community. This will often take the form of verbal abuse and in some cases physical violence. Converts from Hinduism may be obliged to eat separately from the rest of the family and be ostracised in other ways, because to become a Christian is to lose caste and become an outcaste.

The Unfaithful Woman

There are particular problems when a woman renounces her previous religion and comes to faith in Christ in opposition to the rest of the family. In many cultures loyalty to one's husband, at all times, rates very highly. They may have their children taken away from them by angry relatives. Some women choose to remain secret believers. We need to be sensitive to this; not denying Christ's command to witness but perhaps suggesting that they let Jesus show in their behaviour until they are ready to make an open stand.

The Arranged Marriage

In societies where the marriages are arranged by the parents, a young convert will almost certainly have difficulty in finding a partner. The family will try to persuade them to marry someone of their own religion, hoping to bring them back to the family faith. When they suggest one non-Christian partner after another a young person finds it hard to stand firm. Christians should not just stand by and let this happen, but do their utmost to find a Christian partner for them – if possible, one whose background makes them acceptable to the family.

The Loving Community

Converts from another faith need a great deal of love and practical help. If they do not quickly become part of a loving, caring Christian church they may fall away. This is the only community in which they can be nourished in the word of God, grow in faith and Christian understanding and eventually find security. The whole church and not just the minister should be encouraged to help them achieve this goal.

In some cultures people make their own decisions and act independently but in many others family solidarity is very important. In such a culture if the senior member of the family accepts Christ the rest of the family will often follow. Then they will be able to stand together if the wider family and community opposes the stand they have taken.

If you know you are going to a culture where another faith is practised try to find information about it and decide what are the most important of its teachings. Where do these correspond to Christian truths? Where are they different? How do you think you might share your Christian faith in this context?

Prayer

Above all we need to pray for the people we are sharing the gospel with. This is far more important than being able to talk to them skilfully about our Christian faith.

One day a Christian asked a Sikh, "What to you is the most important part of your life as a Sikh?" He replied, "Prayer."

People of all cultures pray, though many only use set forms. They will usually be happy for us to pray with them. If we are able to say a prayer for them and their family in our own words, they will warm to us.

PRACTICAL SUGGESTIONS

Trust the Holy Spirit for your words and actions. He is able to meet every situation and guide every conversation. We are only responsible for witnessing. Convicting anyone that the truth is in Jesus, is the Holy Spirit's responsibility.

Try to put yourself in your friends' shoes enough to understand their problems and objections to the Christian faith.

Avoid using words that do not communicate to the non-Christian, such as atonement, expiation, washed in the blood of the lamb, being born again, sin (some religions regard "sin" as just disobeying the religion's rules), being saved.

Stress the person and purpose of Jesus Christ, and a right relationship between us and God. Christianity is not merely an experience of faith.

Hold fast to the uniqueness of Christ. Many we talk with will object to this, so do not start your friendship by talking about it. However there must come a point under the Holy Spirit's guidance where we do so, even if it means the end of our friendship. Not to make the Christian belief clear is dishonouring to God and in the end not helpful to our friends.

Many religions teach that we must struggle throughout our lives to be accepted by God. We can stress that God reaches out to us with His love and grace.

Never compromise the Christian message.

Stick to a few passages of scripture rather than confusing your friend by hopping all over the Bible.

Look for things in the other faith which may help to explain the gospel.

Share the good news that God is loving and just. Some religions portray God as capricious and needing to be appeased.

Do share your personal experience. Your friends will want to know how God has worked in your life. Tell them how you came to personal faith in Christ. This will help them far more than long explanations of Christian theology.

Don't be afraid to admit you don't know all the answers. Admit you don't know and say you will try to find out. Or you may have to say that we will not know the answer until we get to heaven. In that case we can share the joy and peace of being a Christian and trusting God for what we do not understand.

Make sure you know your Bible well.

Establish the truth that we are sinful. People often believe that people are basically good and are tainted from the outside.

Be aware that your traditional methods and approaches may not be effective.

Be aware that some words will immediately be misunderstood, such as "Son of God" with a Muslim. We need to share the concept that Jesus is God. That's what he claimed for himself.

THE OCCULT

Some animist religions are entirely concerned with gaining the favour of and placating evil spirits. In such a situation the power may be palpable to anyone who enters the culture. It will be obvious that the lives of the people are controlled by the spirit worship.

However in most other religions of the world there are in addition to the normal beliefs and practices many superstitions and occult activities. This is true among people who are nominally Christian, as well as in other faiths. These surface in times of crisis, illness or disaster. People will go to the witch doctor or shaman. In Hinduism meditation and yoga may be practised in order to receive the powers of the gods and use them for oneself.

"Christian" Occult

Even where people have become Christians from other religious backgrounds they may cling to some occult beliefs and practices. Jamaica is a Christian country but there are various groups practising pagan traditions brought from West Africa by the slave trade. They engage in such practices as pocomania which involves sacrificing chickens, or group chanting which works up to fever pitch until someone foams at the mouth, lies raving on the floor, and grunts and groans. This is known as "getting the spirit". The obeah man is powerful in Jamaica and he can be asked to put a spell on someone else for evil purposes or be pleaded with to grant powers through spells.

TAKE CHRIST'S AUTHORITY

If we find ourselves in a society where the occult plays any part the first thing we must do is stand in the Lord's victory. He is more powerful than anything evil and He gives us authority in Christ to "bind" evil powers and "loose" people subject to them. We should positively take this authority and not just assume it is there.

DESTROY THE OBJECTS

It is most important to teach young Christians to renounce the occult and destroy any objects in their possession which are connected with it. If we are not clear whether certain actions, sensations, or illnesses are the work of the evil one, we should ask God for the gift of the discernment of spirits. He has promised this to those who need it. If we move into a house affected by the occult, we should go from room to room destroying any signs of occult practice and asking Jesus to cleanse it, destroy the evil power and protect the room and whoever uses it.

PRAY FOR PROTECTION

When we first arrive in a new country we may be fascinated by the ceremonies of other faiths and want to pay visits to temples and shrines. It is advisable not to make a practice of this, though we may want to observe occasionally to learn what goes on. If we do we should pray for protection in Christ before we go, from any power of evil which uses the ceremonies. It is important to realise that a demon's power is real and we can be vulnerable to the spiritual depression which can result.

BE SAFE "IN CHRIST"

But we should not go to another culture in fear and trembling about facing the power of evil. We are "in Christ" and as long as we remain there we are safe and can go out and do battle in His name as and when necessary.

RELATING TO OTHER FAITHS

Bill Houston

Christian faith claims to be universally true with respect to its revelation of God, the means and nature of salvation and God's purposes for the world. The best and shortest summary of this position is the early Christian confession that 'Jesus Christ is Lord'. It creates a problem. 'One of the most difficult and crucial theological problems before the church today is understanding the lordship of Jesus Christ over a world that is religiously plural' (Anderson & Stransky, *Christ's Lordship and Religious Pluralism*).

People in primal religious societies do not have this problem. Their beliefs are closely linked to the limited geographical area in which they live. They claim no universality nor do they have a missionary vision. But the missionary vision is part of the very nature of the church. 'As fire is to burning so mission is to the Church,' said Emil Brunner.

Our God is a missionary God — he sent his Son. The Son is a missionary Son — he and the Father sent the Holy Spirit. The Spirit is a Missionary Spirit — he calls out and sends Christians into the world to bear witness to Jesus and to glorify God. Mission is therefore part of the very nature of the Trinity. It is in going out into the world that the issue of inter-faith encounter arises.

The church has always had to grapple with the challenge of relating to other religions. The early church, for instance, had to sort out its relationship to Judaism, then to the religions of the Graeco-Roman world, to the mystery religions of the Middle East and to gnosticism. This challenge is not novel to the twentieth century, but it has grown in importance; people are more aware of many other religions than ever before.

A growing awareness

Increased international travel on business trips or holidays has brought Westerners into close personal contact with people of different faiths. Buddhism, Islam and Hinduism can be seen at first hand. As people are forced to take them seriously, they may start to re-evaluate the Christian faith as well.

Immigration into the West, and the presence of guest workers or refugees from abroad, has changed the religious composition of many countries. In the UK, Leicester has the second largest Hindu community outside of India. Some two hundred thousand Sikhs now live in Britain and there are almost six million Muslims in the Common Market countries. It is not unusual today to see mosques in British cities. In some schools Gentiles ('Christians') are in a minority. Teachers of religious education confronted the problem of teaching Christian truth in a multi-religious context long before most clergy even put it on their agendas.

In multi-ethnic and plurally religious societies it is vitally important to foster understanding and good will. The world needs inter-religious cooperation to tackle the universal concerns of a war-weary humanity

struggling for social justice, mere survival and world harmony. Many therefore suggest that it would be unwise to cause dissension and bad feeling by preaching the gospel. It seems difficult for a local church to hold together the twin poles of good neighbourliness and evangelistic zeal.

Western education has taught people more about other religions, and made them aware of the similarities and differences, the fascinating approaches to spirituality, and the various ethical emphases such as Mahatma Gandhi's non-violent approach. Sometimes this

creates an awareness of the failings of our own culture. How secularised the West has become! How materialistic! Things are put before people. When we reflect on the slaughter during two world wars, how barbarous! When we think on the high divorce rate with the many emotionally scarred children, how sad!

The end of the colonial era and the decline of European colonial powers has been matched by the rise of assertive, independent national states. In some of them — such as Islamic states — religion forms the cornerstone of the national identity. 'Non-Christian' countries also exert financial muscle; oil-rich Arabian states, and Japan, Korea and Taiwan are conspicuous examples. The unconscious link in people's minds between the supremacy of the gospel and the power of Western 'culture', technology, force of arms and economics is now no longer valid. Was it Christianity that made the Western nations great? If so, then given their relative decline, is not the entire Christian mission also under suspicion? This line of thinking has undermined some Christians' convictions about the validity of Christian mission.

Another corrosive influence has been the loss of confidence in the scriptures. 'Thanks to negative biblical criticism and to the pressures of secular thinking in the West, Western Christians have grown uncertain of their own faith' (editorial, *Themelios*, IFES, Jan. 1984). Some people are so unsure of the claims of scripture that they have become universalists, believing that all religious teaching can be put on an equal footing.

What is more, non-Christian religions today are more missionary-minded. We are on the receiving end of other people's missionary outreach! Hinduism is no longer confined to India. The Ramakrishna mission has centres in many countries. In the late 1960s and 1970s many disillusioned people went east in search of a meaning to life. Zen-Buddhism is found in the

West. Islam is particularly energetic in propagating its faith. Even the traditional tribal religions, from which most Christian converts have been made, are creatively responding to modernity by revising, adapting and sustaining their religions.

In 1913 a German missiologist, Johannes Warneck, observed in his book *The Living Christ and Dying Heathenism* that paganism appeared to be in its death throes. The optimistic mood of the 1910 world missionary conference in Edinburgh has proved to be mistaken.

The net result of all this is that the Christian faith is generally seen as one among equals in the forum of world religions. It means that some Christians have lost their missionary nerve and they question the whole missionary enterprise.

On the other hand there have been some benefits. Authentic mission has been stripped of its imperialistic or paternalistic superiority complex. This chastened mood permits mission to follow more closely the pattern demonstrated in Jesus the suffering servant. The rapid rise in the number of Third World Christians who have gone as cross-cultural missionaries (one study suggests a total of over 20,000 non-Western missionaries) will in time remove the stigma which associates the gospel with Western culture, and will demonstrate the universal nature of the church called out by our global God for a worldwide task.

It is clear, therefore, that the relationship between Christianity and other world faiths is a hot issue today. Any Christian who plans to live in the context of another religion must sort out his/her approach to other religions.

Five possible approaches to other religions

The variety of attitudes to other religions may confuse the newcomer to this subject. This variety arises from different approaches to the scriptures, and different personal encounters with other religions. Even classifying the schools of thought is not easy because one group may overlap with another; the spectrum of thought ranges from a radical discontinuity between Christianity and other religions through a continuity between them.

1. Radical discontinuity

Christianity is the only true religion and all other religions are fake, according to this approach. Other religions are the product of sin which has marred any original revelation there might have been, and the work of Satan who has blinded the eyes of their devotees. It follows that the Christian has nothing to learn from them. There is no continuity whatsoever between God's revelation in Christ and non-Christian religions. The early Christian apologist, Tertullian, championed this approach. 'What has Athens to do with Jerusalem?' he said. People suppress the truth of God's revelation by their wickedness and exchange the truth of God for a lie. They are without excuse and are therefore guilty before God, people who hold this view would say.

Karl Barth is a modern exponent of this view. He, however, believed that any religion (including Christianity insofar as it is the result of human effort) is in fact an expression of man's flight from God.

2. Preparation for Christ

Christianity does not come to destroy but to fulfil and complete, it is suggested. It is only in Christ that other religions find their fulfilment. This approach suggests that just as the Old Testament law and practice of Judaism was a preparation for Christ's coming even though it was inadequate in itself, so too God is using the other world faiths in a similar way. Their partial insights are corrected and completed by the gospel.

Some early Christian apologists (Irenaeus and Origen) argued this way with respect of the great Greek philosophers. They reinterpreted the Greek 'logos' idea and linked it to Jesus, the Logos of the New Testament. The result was a positive evaluation of non-Christian religions.

Later on, evolutionary theories inferred that 'lower' religions need to develop into a higher form, namely Christianity. A classic statement of this is found in a book written in 1913 by J N Farquhar, *The Crown of Hinduism*. For him Christianity was the crown of Hinduism.

3. Both continuity and discontinuity

Calvin taught on the basis of Romans 1 that all people have some sense of deity which is seen through creation, history and conscience. Even debased people retain some germ of true religion (*semen religionis*). There is nevertheless a huge gulf between this 'natural religion' and the 'special revelation' of God in Christ which alone is sufficient for salvation. It follows that other religions might have some true elements but that there is no salvation outside of Christ.

4. Redemption analogies

A recent innovative approach is taken by Don Richardson, the author of *Peace Child*. In his book *Eternity in Their Hearts* he writes of 'startling evidence of belief in the one true God in hundreds of cultures throughout the world'. God has not left himself without a witness (Acts 14:17) but in every culture there are stories or practices which Christians may use as redemptive analogies and form the basis for preaching the gospel. While the non-Christian religion does not teach the true way of salvation it does contain elements which may be used as bridges between the preaching of Christ and the 'pagan' religion.

5. The Roman Catholic view
The encyclical *Ecclesiam Suam* (1964) arranges religions in a series of concentric circles with the Roman Catholic Church at the centre followed by other Christians, Jews, Muslims, other theists, other religions and atheists.

Roman Catholic theology, having been influenced by Thomas Aquinas's distinction between 'nature' and 'grace', has traditionally had a more sympathetic evaluation of other natural religions. More recently theologians such as Karl Rahner have argued that non-Christian religions are the ordinary paths to salvation, while the Christian religion is the extraordinary way. It is therefore possible to regard adherents of these religions as 'anonymous Christians'.

From awareness to dialogue
It will be clear that each of the approaches outlined above can have a profound impact on the aims and methods of mission. You would do well to read Lesslie Newbigin's critique of the various positions in his book *The Open Secret*. We do not have the space to consider the universalistic approaches which teach that all religions are but different paths to a single truth. The paths might be religious, philosophical, mystical, moralistic or cultural but in each case they attempt to equate Christianity with other religions with each having equally valid but partial insights.

Attitudes affect our actions. The Christian must examine him or herself for any attitudes of racism, paternalism or a sense of superiority. Christians going abroad are to be ambassadors of Christ and his gospel, and not agents of Western culture, capitalism or technology. We will be living letters seen and read by the nationals. As ambassadors of the gospel we need to be marked by the gospel. These attributes should characterise our encounters with people of other faiths.

The 'in' word is dialogue. John Stott in his *Christian Mission in the Modern World* lays out four marks of true dialogue. First, there is the

mark of personal *authenticity*. We need to be seen to be real human beings who are genuine in our love. We are, like others, equally sinful, equally needy, and equally dependent on the grace of God. The other person is a human being too, not just an object (or soul) to be evangelised. Dialogue is a true meeting of person to person. Dialogue puts evangelism into an authentically human context. The apostle Paul beautifully summarises this in 1 Thessalonians 2:7-8: 'But we were gentle among you, like a mother caring for her little children. We loved you so much that we were delighted to share with you not only the gospel of God but our lives as well, because you had become so dear to us.'

Secondly, true dialogue carries the mark of *humility*. As we listen to people we respect them as human beings made in the image of God. We cannot unfeelingly dismiss their point of view, nor should we try to win debating points. Some of their misconceptions may be our fault, or the fault of Christian errors in the past, or because they have a mis-shapen caricature of Christ. Yes, they may be in error, but so were we once. The Holy Spirit first convicts us, and through us convicts the world. We go as beggars telling other beggars where to find bread. Do not try to defend the embarrassing errors of Christianity as a religion – the crusades, the passivity of the church during the holocaust, the theological justification of apartheid, the fact that the church is part of the problem and not the solution in Ireland and elsewhere. With due humility point beyond all that to Jesus. Humility in evangelism is a beautiful grace.
Thirdly, true dialogue has a mark of *integrity*. We need to listen in order to understand the real beliefs of the other person. At the end you should be able to say 'As I understand you, this is what you believe...' And they will say, 'Yes, that is correct.' This is what you would expect of others yourself. You need not agree with their position, but at least you will have an accurate understanding of their belief structures and be able to bring the word of God to bear in your reply. Our preconceived notions and our false images will be changed. You will be changed: be ready for that!

Sources of information on other religions include: their prayers, holy books, priests and holy people, oral tradition, rituals, holy places, religious art and music, taboos and prohibitions. Try to understand their world-view. What questions are they trying to answer?

What issues in life are they facing? What are their presuppositions about the world, people, evil, life, death, time, ethics, and so forth?

Fourthly, true dialogue is marked by *sensitivity*. Stott writes, 'Christian evangelism falls into disrepute when it degenerates into stereotypes. It is impossible to evangelise by fixed formulae. To force a conversation along predetermined lines in order to reach a predetermined destination is to show oneself grievously lacking in sensitivity, both to the actual needs of our friend, and to the guidance of the Holy Spirit. Such insensitivity is therefore a failure in both faith and love.'

Note that dialogue does not mean that Christians should hide or suspend their beliefs. Far from it, to be authentic, a Christian must declare the truths which are precious to him or her. Dialogue, in fact, will stimulate Christians to a deeper understanding of their faith in Christ in order to answer the searching questions posed by the partner in dialogue.

The time will come when there will be a fundamental clash in beliefs. When claims to truth compete you should be able to explain reasonably four things:

1. The authority and inspiration of God's revealed Word.

2. The uniqueness of Jesus as the incarnate Born of God who died to atone for sin and rose again from the dead. The message of the gospel is not about 'religion', but about a Person, and the question boils down to 'What do you think about Christ?'

3. That the purpose of salvation is inclusive, but God's means of salvation is exclusively in Christ.

4. That God by his Holy Spirit has woven a thread of sacred history through his covenant people in the Old Testament, and through members of the kingdom of God as bearers of the gospel in 'the last days'.

One cannot be a disciple of Jesus Christ and not engage in the struggle for truth. The New Testament calls us to 'convince', 'convict' or 'rebuke'. Other religions are inadequate vehicles of salvation, and must be shown to be so. People need to have sin unmasked and to be led to repentance and faith in Christ.

LEARNING ABOUT RELIGION

CONTENTS

PURPOSE

This Unit will help you in your overall approach to other religions and encourage you to learn more about one of them.

THE PUZZLE OF PLURALISM

"There are elements of truth [in other religions] which must come from God himself, whether through the memory of an original revelation... or through some measure of self-disclosure... to those who truly seek Him. But there are also elements which are definitely false. ... Yet again, there is much that could best be described as human aspirations after the truth..."

Sir Norman Anderson

The Shorter Oxford Dictionary defines pluralism as

"a system of thought which recognises more than one ultimate principle"

Brian Hill, a specialist in Religious Education, defines it as

"an individual state of mind whereby one is sensitive to the problematic status of all systems of belief and value given the plurality of options now presented to human consciousness in the global village"

Both of these definitions illustrate that pluralism exists wherever there are fundamental and unresolvable differences of opinion over issues of belief or values. Most people respond to this situation by putting on blinkers – they either ignore the differences of opinion, or dismiss those who disagree with them as intellectually or morally inferior.

Pluralism is a fact of life in modern Britain. That would be true even without the presence of religions other than Christianity. There is pluralism in the church when Christians disagree over fundamental aspects of belief – say over whether the Resurrection is myth or historical event.

We have to take on board the strength of the following points:

- There is a great diversity of religious commitment, both in Britain and in the world at large. There is no getting away from it.

- These religious commitments are very strongly held. They are the shaping forces in people's lives. It is religious belief that so often gives meaning to an individual's existence. So each commitment needs to be treated with the utmost respect.

- We cannot resolve these differences by accumulating more evidence or thinking more rationally. In the final analysis people have to agree to differ.

- The health of a plural society depends on people learning to live together and respect each other's rights, without feeling they are compromising their own deeply held beliefs.

The problem for many Christians is that their beliefs are in the final analysis exclusivist. Ultimately they want to say that Jesus Christ is the only way to God. Other Christians put such emphasis on affirming other people's insights that in the end it amounts to saying that each person's religious beliefs are true for them if they have been arrived at through an insight experience. That is essentially pluralist. The widely used parable of the blind man and the elephant is an example of this (see *The World Christian* page 73).

We have to live with the tension between accepting the absolute claims of Jesus Christ and genuinely accepting that all have the freedom to believe what they choose.

Many Christians feel themselves caught in a theological dilemma. Do they have to let go of their "exclusivist" Christian beliefs if they are to be a "responsible" person in the plural context? I believe it is possible to remain true to an "exclusivist" Christian position while at the same time:

■ affirming that there are aspects of truth in other religions and common values shared between religions

■ affirming and respecting the right of other people to hold beliefs incompatible with Christianity

It is a fact that different people hold different religious beliefs. We are more aware of this in today's world, where people from all parts of the world mix more freely than ever before. We often hear it said that we are living in a "pluralist world" or "pluralist society", in which everybody has the right and opportunity to choose how they wish to believe and live. We are told that "religions and cultural pluralism" are the marks of our age.

We need to be careful how we use these terms. "Pluralism" is a slippery word, which means different things to different people.

■ Some use it just to refer to the fact which we have already noted, that many different beliefs and viewpoints exist side by side.

■ Others use it to mean that these different beliefs are all of equal validity. None can be said to be absolutely or exclusively true. They are all true in a relative sense.

Plurality

To avoid confusion, it seems better to use the word plurality to describe the fact of different views. Christians should be the first to acknowledge this and to welcome the idea of freedom of choice and tolerance for all views. Because we believe that God the Creator has made us all different and has given us the amazing freedom to search for Him and hold our own views (as Paul says in Acts 17.27). So we accept the plurality of religious (and cultural and political) views in our society.

That is not the same as pluralism in the sense that all these views are relative, or different aspects of the truth, or equally valid.

If we believe that the good news is that God has revealed Himself uniquely in Jesus Christ, then we believe that this is the ultimate truth by which all our efforts to find the truth are to be judged. There is such a thing as absolute truth, by which we assess the varying truth claims. (That is not to say that our particular interpretation or exposition of God's truth has absolute status: we can be, and often are, mistaken).

This is how Ajith Fernando sums up Paul's attitude:

"On the one hand there is a firm belief in the wrongness of life apart from Christ. On the other hand there is a respect for all individuals because they are intelligent human beings endowed by God with the privilege and responsibility of choosing to accept or reject the gospel. This caused Paul to reason with them about the truth of God. This combination of a strong conviction about truth and a respect for the individual ... forms one of the foundational principles in formulating our attitude to other faiths."

Much of the material on pages 72-73 is by Trevor Cooling.

We can and must listen to others, understand their views, reason with them, and witness to the truth that we have experienced. And we must do so with sensitivity and respect, remembering that we are dealing with the things which are most precious and valuable to any person – their deepest beliefs and aspirations, hopes and fears. Our purpose is to understand, to respect, to relate to people of other faiths than our own.

FURTHER READING

The World's Religions (Lion), pages 10-18 "The Study of Religion", pages 357-363 "The Claim to be Unique".
The World's Religions (IVP), chapter "A Christian Approach to Comparative Religion".
Who is my Neighbour? pages 7-28.
(See page 78 for more details)

VARIETIES OF PLURALISM

Paul Schrotenboer

Introduction

Without variety life would be monotonous, uninteresting, poor. Variety gives richness, potentiality and flavour to life. It is, we say, the spice of life. Dr. Abraham Kuyper referred to this aspect of our experience when in 1869 he declared that 'uniformity is the curse of modern life'. Among the many ideas he advocated was that of pluriformity. He applied it both to church and to state.

Life's variety not only gives pleasure but also produces tensions and conflicts, for with many differences we do not know how to cope in a calm and peaceful way. All too often they lead to open strife and permanent alienation.

A word much in use today to express differences is 'pluralism', a term that itself has a variety of contexts and connotations. The term 'pluralism' is often used imprecisely, without reference to the context in which it is used. When this happens the reader does not always know what the writer had in mind.

Another closely related term is 'plurality'. The difference between plurality and pluralism is that the latter is too much of a good thing. What this means should become apparent in what follows.

Another term closely related to pluralism is 'toleration'. The two terms differ, in that toleration describes an *attitude* which allows for differences, and pluralism refers to a *settled argument* where toleration and equality prevail.

The fact that we can speak of the many kinds of pluralism, and that it affects so many life zones, indicates that our society as a whole is pluralist. The sameness that once characterized our societies has largely disappeared.

Pluralism is seen by some as an evil to be eradicated where it exists and a plague to be avoided where it has not yet put in an appearance. Others see pluralism as the most just arrangement that society can hope for and believe it must exist not only in society but also in the church if harmony is to prevail.

It is the aim of this essay to demonstrate the need to distinguish clearly between areas or life zones of human existence in order to evaluate how pluralism functions in each. Pluralism in politics is quite different from pluralism in the church and our evaluation will differ accordingly. Moreover neither cultural or religious pluralism (both of which cover the entire spectrum of human existence) can be subsumed under 'politics'. In this essay we shall limit our comments to culture, religion, and politics.

Cultural pluralism

Christianity from its inception has been a multi-cultural religion. As such it differs from its predecessor Judaism which was tied to the Hebrew culture. Not exclusively, for the Old Testament writings were translated in about the year 200 BC into Greek in what came to be called the Septuagint, the first translation of the Bible into a vernacular language.

At Pentecost the gospel was proclaimed in all sixteen languages which were represented by the people gathered at the feast in Jerusalem. This was not the result of a grand scheme of the disciples of Jesus; it occurred by fiat of the Holy Spirit who gave the gift of tongues to the followers of Jesus. Pentecost was the decisive breakthrough of the mono-cultural religion of the followers of Abraham whom God had singled out, separated for centuries from the other peoples of the world, preserved through many dynasties and finally used as the vehicle to bring forth the Christ who would become the Saviour and Judge of all nations, not just one.

Not only would the message of Jesus and the resurrection be proclaimed in all the languages of the then world, but people of every tongue would be accepted into the Christian church on an equal footing. This was the lesson Peter had to learn in his encounter with Cornelius at Joppa (Acts 10) and the entire church was led to accept (when it seemed good to the Holy Spirit and to them) that Jew and Gentile should be accorded equal status in the new fellowship of people who were saved by grace, not by performing works prescribed by law (Acts 15).

Again, this was not a discovery of the leaders of the early church. It was rather a conviction forced upon them by the Spirit of God in special revelation, much against their will. At Joppa Peter was finally convinced that when God made all foods clean his truth was marching on beyond the earlier particularism (for Jews only) to take into his saving arms people of every nation. Only then was Peter ready to baptize Gentile believers. How could he argue against the coming of the Spirit upon the band of followers of the way in Cornelius' house?

What the church experienced already at Pentecost it has continued to put into practice. Nowhere, perhaps, does this appear more clearly than in the way in which the oral reports of the life and sayings of Jesus and of the early expansion of the church was recorded. Jesus had spoken in Aramaic, the everyday language of the Jews after the Exile, but when his disciples wrote the Gospels and the Apostles sent their letters to the young churches, they wrote them all in Greek. At that very early age it became apparent that the new movement that was based on the life and teaching of Jesus of Nazareth would not be limited to the Hebrew and Aramaic languages which only a small percentage of the people in the Roman Empire spoke. The vehicle of transmission for the Good News was the world language, namely *koine* Greek.

That Greek would be the language of the church for only a short while, and that even at that time only partially, was already decided at Pentecost when the gospel was heard by the people, everyone in his or her own language. The church took its cue from Pentecost and, following the Holy Spirit's example, has continued to proclaim the gospel in the vernacular languages. Even the hold of Latin upon the Roman Catholic Church has in recent times been broken.

This stress on using every language as a vehicle of transmitting the gospel has characterized the church until this day and has been most prominent in those circles which stress transcultural evangelism. The need to translate the Scriptures into the many languages was even elevated to a part of the church's confession in the Westminster Confession of Faith (I, viii).

Prof. Lamim Sanneh makes the point in 'Pluralism and Christian Commitment' (*Theology Today*, April 1988) that Christian commitment is compatible with genuine pluralism. He observes that the translation work of the Christian missionary movement has led to the Scriptures being presented in more than 1,800 languages. The *missio Dei* is not in conflict with but consistent with the maintaining of cultural integrity. 'In centring on the primacy of God's word, Christian translators invested the vernacular with consecrated power, lifting obscure tribes to the level of scriptural heritage and into the stream of universal world history' (p. 27). Says he, 'If the argument is pressed that mission was wrong because it interfered with the cultures of others, then the evidence on the ground that mission in fact bolstered indigenous cultures should be sufficient to answer it' (p. 29)

It must be granted that for many decades the Protestant mission was reluctant to use the entire culture of the receptor people and in fact often imposed elements of the culture of the missionary, but of recent time it has become apparent that God uses every culture as an instrument not only to transmit but to live the Gospel. Today the principle that there is no absolute culture that is normative for all others is working through to relativize Western culture which has been the garb that has clothed most of the trans-cultural mission work done in the past few centuries. Few still claim that people in the Third World need to be westernized when they declare themselves disciples of Jesus Christ.

With its stance of a multi-cultural transmission of the Christian message, of relativizing the Hebrew, Greek and Western cultures, the Christian religion stands in contrast to both modern Judaism and Islam. Orthodox Jews still insist on the priority of Hebrew; Muslims on Arabic. In the Synagogue and in the Mosque only the sacred languages are legitimate. No Christians are allowed to visit the Islamic holy city Mecca.

The Christian religion stands out among the other world religions as one that holds that Christian

HERE YOU ARE - YOU CAN BORROW MY MATCHES !...

commitment to God, the faith of Jesus Christ, involves commitment to cultural forms in their essentially plural relativism. Christian commitment, as Sanneh says, is thus rewarded with a cultural pluralism of the most lively and diverse kind (p. 32).

The importance of recognizing cultural pluralism in the transmission of the gospel may be seen in the fact that culture (which is the product of human communal work that gives form to the way we live) shapes both the tongue that tells and the ear that hears the gospel. It is the indispensable vehicle of communicating the Good News. It is that whole social environment in which and through which we seek to obey the truth of the gospel.

When the gospel comes to a people and they respond to it, the Good News impacts on the culture in two ways: it judges it by purging it of unacceptable elements and it transforms it, making it a fit instrument for the Master's use. The gospel, as it were, takes possession of the culture.

Because of the dual impact of judgement and transformation, there can be no identification of the gospel with one or other culture (for here the medium is not the message), nor can the culture of the receptor people be by-passed in bringing the gospel.

Space does not permit us to go into greater detail on how gospel and culture interact. But it should be clear that pluralism in culture is not an obstacle to be deplored, but an opportunity to be grasped.

Pluralism in religion

The word religion usually refers to institutions and acts of worship. Sometimes it is used as a synonym for the church. As such it is one of several areas of life. At times it is understood as one of two fundamental life-dimensions, called the 'sacred'. It is then contrasted with 'nature', the secular area. Neither of these meanings is what we have in mind.

Religion as we now speak of it is that broad-as-life directedness of human existence that forces human beings to deal with God and his revelation and to serve him, or whatever or whoever takes his place.

This comprehensive meaning of religion was understood by the monastics who joined together in religious orders which controlled every aspect of their lives. But over time this comprehensive usage fell into disuse and religion was reduced to a part of human experience and later reduced even more to one institution among many.

Religion as we speak of it is service, response. Man himself is not a substance, that is, something which, as Descartes said, needs nothing outside of himself to exist, but a response being, totally and permanently dependent upon the God who made him, continues to uphold him and will one day call him to give account.

The Scriptures speak of man as the image of God. And whatever else this word conveys, it means that man is not self-existent but the reflection and representative of his Maker. It is instructive to note that the Genesis story tells us both that God made Adam and Eve in his image and that Adam had a son in his image, Seth (Genesis 5:3). Thus just as Adam could take his son in his arms and see that he looked like his father, so God could observe Adam as he was busy in the garden and see in him a reflection of himself.

Religion in this full, authentic sense means the total commitment and service of man. It is not one kind of activity along side of others, nor is it one area of life in the midst of other areas; in its God-directedness it is a way of life. Life is religion, *Gottesdienst*.

Plurality in religion means that there is in humanity a variety of total commitments: e.g. the Christian, the Hindu, the Islamic, the Buddhist, the humanist, African traditional religions and others.

Religious plurality has been a fact of life since humankind was early differentiated between the 'children of God' and the 'sons of man' (Genesis 6:1,2). From the beginning man has had the tendency to turn from God to idols. From the worship of idols God called Abraham; from the worship of them God continued to call his people: 'You shall have no other gods before me' (Exodus 20:3; Deut 5:7).

Religious pluralism (which as we shall note is not the same as plurality of religions) has become a topic for much discussion in recent time for a number of reasons. One of these is the recent mixing of people. Time was when people lived and remained in areas where nearly all the inhabitants held the same religious commitment. Thus the Hindus lived in India, the Muslims in the Islamic lands and the adherents of African traditional religion in their own part of Africa. For centuries in Europe after the Reformation Catholics tended to live in areas with a Catholic government and Protestants in Protestant lands. The one exception was the Jews who were scattered around the world in the diaspora; but even they tended to congregate in their own neighbourhoods. Today, thanks in large part to Western colonialism, the Christian mission and modern transportation, adherents of opposing religions exist side by side not only in the universities of all Western lands but in a society as a whole. This movement of people goes far to explain why religious pluralism has become so prominent as an issue today.

In the West the prevailing attitude is: live and let live. Each religious community has equal right to the benefits of society along with other communities. It was not always so, nor is it true in every country today. In the time of the early church Caesar claimed that he was God and required of all his subjects to recognize that claim. At that time the Christians advanced the counter claim that Jesus is Lord and many paid the supreme sacrifice for that confession (cf. Acts 17:7 for a direct reference to the conflict).

When in the beginning of the Constantine era (4th. century) Christianity was made the official religion of the Roman Empire, the roles were reversed. Now the adherents of the non-Christian religions were given second rate status. They were tolerated but not considered equal.

Later, after the 16th. century Reformation, the idea prevailed for a century or so that every land should have its own religion (e.g. Catholic, Lutheran, Reformed). Accordingly, people who did not share the religion required by the rulers could either convert, or leave, or stay and suffer the consequences.

Today there is not only a mixing of religious communities in the West, but also a resurgence of non-Christian religions. At the turn of this century the other religions were seen to be in retreat and the widely held expectation was that eventually they would lose their vitality and strength, and all the while the Christian religion would advance.

That idea gets little support today. The power of the Islamic states, in which religion and politics are coextensive, is enough to convince one that Islam is undergoing a resurgence, with the help of petro-dollars. Likewise, Buddhism and Hinduism enjoy new life and engage in counter mission. Today on all sides the Christian religion is under attack — from atheistic governments, from secularists, from other religions.

We shall not at this time enter further into the practice by the state to determine or influence religion. That comes up for discussion under the section on pluralism in politics. What we should note, however, is that idea that now enjoys great strength in Western society, namely that the various world religions are all equally valid. No claim to truth can be considered absolute. This is what is usually meant by the term religious pluralism. It raises the issue whether there are many roads that lead to the Kingdom of God.

Some years ago a book appeared in the USA under the title: *Christ's Lordship and Religious Pluralism.* It considers the question, How can Christianity, which claims universality for its vision of God and confesses Christ's lordship over the world, live as one religious community among others which possess their own particular faith and truth claims? To this question answers are given by sixteen contributors of various theological orientations.

One answer to the question of religious pluralism comes in the form of syncretism, a position that would advance the mixing of religions, advocating in its most developed form the formation of one great world religion by incorporating into it elements of all the existing world religions.

The classic example of syncretism is the Pantheon in Rome. In this temple there is room for all the gods, but only if they all renounce the claim of exclusive access to ultimate deity and final truth.

This idea has been given more recent form in the Baha'i religion which originated in Persia and has erected its great nine-sided temple in Wilmette, Illinois, each side representing one of the great world religions. It will come as no surprise that the Baha'is have been persecuted in the Middle East by the Islamic state of Iran.

It is becoming popular to say that passages in the Bible (such as that Jesus is the only Way, that his is the only Name, that he is the one Mediator, the only Foundation and that his sacrifice of himself was once and for all time) are true for those who espouse the Christian faith. These affirmations must be understood, so it is said, as the 'language of love'. Thus, a young man may say to his bride 'You are the most beautiful woman in the World', and he means it. So too, the claim that Jesus is the one and only way to God is valid and true for Christians; but the adherent of another religion can make equal claims for the founder of that faith too.

In similar vein the Roman Catholic theologian Paul Knitter claims that since the New Testament writings were written in the expectation of the early return of Jesus Christ, all expressions about the finality of Christ were 'culturally limited'. Gregory Baum, also Roman Catholic, describes the exclusive claims as 'survival dogma', the language of power and domination. It is strange that the efforts to escape the force of the New Testament message of the exclusive lordship of

Jesus Christ can diverge so greatly as to call them in one instance the language of love and in another the language of domination.

We shall resist the inclination to consider at this time the question of whether the lostness of people who do not confess Christ as Saviour and Lord is compatible with the Bible's emphasis on the love of God. Suffice it to say that the Bible itself does not make a problem of what to many seems to be a contradiction.

Space does not permit us either to consider further the question of the conflict of various truth claims. Nor can we comment on the influence of the idea of truth as relational in a subjectivist sense; and on whether such a view that *a priori* claims one religion to be true, and all others utterly false, has full biblical support.

We would observe that if the idea of religious pluralism takes hold, it will spell the demise of the Christian mission. Religious pluralism, we may conclude, is one kind that we would be most reluctant to accept.

In review, we may observe that religious *plurality* refers to the fact that there are many fundamentally different answers to the questions of human existence. A question we should consider in the section on political pluralism is how the different religious communities can live in civil peaceful coexistence.

Proponents of religious *pluralism* hold that these fundamental differences do not *as truth claims* mutually exclude one another. Those who oppose religious pluralism but recognize religious plurality hold that there can be no peaceful coexistence among conflicting claims of truth. They hold that the particularity of the Christian revelation is an essential aspect of the *skandalon* of the gospel.

Political pluralism

The state is one of the public sectors in which the affairs of life in society are to be regulated by justice and are enforced by penalty and the sword. The state enjoys the right of coercion. The regulation of civil affairs is called politics or statecraft.

There is a similarity between religion and the state, namely that both are inescapable. We have observed earlier that, as the image of God, human beings cannot but respond to God in one way or other. Likewise, as inhabitants in a legal jurisdiction or state, one can choose to go from one state to another, but not from a state to a stateless condition.

This involuntary character of our involvement in the state (we are willy nilly a part of one civil jurisdiction or other) means that if there is to be true freedom and justice for all, then there must be a plurality of political options, including the exercise of religion. The Muslim, the Jew, the Christian, the Humanist, the Buddhist and the atheist should all be accorded equal rights before the law.

This is not to say that all the opposing religious claims are as such equally valid; but it *is* to say that in a just society there must be the freedom to exercise all religions, provided that such exercise does not infringe upon the civil rights of others. A just state with a mono-religious stance is a contradiction in terms. Social justice also means that no one religion may enjoy preference over another.

The view that most adequately expresses the way in which equality of rights and opportunity may be protected for all religious groups and individuals is appropriately called 'principled pluralism'.

The society regulated by principled pluralism differs from the Islamic (sacral) state which wipes out the distinction between state and church. It must also be distinguished from the modern secular state which in the name of 'separation of church and state' seeks to abolish all influence and even the symbols of religion (the Cross, the Star of David, the Minaret) from public life. As a reaction against the infringement of the church upon the affairs of the state, adherents of the secular state seek to grant equality to all by putting the public sector out of bounds to all religions.

This view has the advantage that it grants to no religious body preference over another. It allows for no establishment of religion. In the secular society there will be no religious wars.

The flaw in this view is that, having identified religion in effect with church and cultic activities, it does not permit any expression of religion in public life. The result is a 'naked public square'.

The shortcomings of 'principled pluralism' are truly serious, for by seeking to restrict all manifestations of religion to the private sectors of church and home (and school if the parents are willing — and able — to pay double) the proponents are advocating what may be called the 'religion of secular humanism'.

As we noted earlier, man's response to God

(or that which functions in his place — an idol) irresistibly functions in every sector of life, including the public sector, whether we are willing to recognize it or not. The idea of the secular state is one such response.

A prime *tenet of faith* of secular humanism is that in the really important area of life, where men and women make a living and decide the issues of society, people manage much better if they leave all their ideas of God at home. No less than the recognized religions, the unrecognized religion of secular humanism seeks to give answers to the fundamental questions of human existence. The basic conviction that man can manage best by keeping God out of public life functions as a control belief, determining what people may and may not do.

The idea of principled pluralism in politics accepts neither the idea of the sacral state, nor the halfway house that, while tolerating all, grants to one religion or denomination preference over others. It stands for full equality in civil affairs for adherents of all religions, without exception.

Nor does this kind of pluralism in statecraft opt for a secular state, which is a greater threat in the West today than the kind of politics that identifies church and state. It advocates a pluralism that is based on the principle of justice for all, in all life zones.

The basic principle is that people should exercise their religiously directed civil responsibilities in such a way that the free exercise of religion is not denied or restricted. The alternative to having to go either the way of the sacral state or the secular state is to give each and every faith community equal right and opportunity as well in public as in private. The mosque, the synagogue, the temple, and the church should all enjoy equal rights before the law. Muslims, Jews, Christians and Humanists should all share equally in tax money for education. Institutions for meeting social needs should all receive equal public protection and support, whether they are of one or other religious conviction or claim to have no faith at all. Where the policies of principled pluralism are put into effect a truly pluralist and just society can exist.

Reprinted from The Reformed Ecumenical Council Theological Forum, November 1988.

WHICH RELIGION?

At this point you need to choose which religion you are going to study with a view to meeting a person of that faith. If you are already in contact with someone of another faith, or know that you want to live and witness amongst people of a particular faith, then this may make up your mind for you. In practical terms though there may be a tension between a religious faith you are interested in and the religious communities you have access to. The process is more important than the knowledge of a particular faith; so choose what is practical. What you learn in this module can be transferred to people of another faith community.

You will need a resource book, and I suggest one of the following:

- Lion Handbook, *The World's Religions*, Lion Publishing, 1982. This is the most comprehensive and detailed of the one volume books on world religions.

- J.N.D. Anderson (ed.), *The World's Religions*, IVP, 1984. A good basic survey, with a helpful chapter at the end on our approach to other religions. But it has nothing on Sikhism.

- Martin Goldsmith and Rosemary Harley, *Who Is My Neighbour?*, Scripture Union, 1988. Short and simply written, but by no means simplistic. It has a section of good material on new religious movements, both Eastern and Western.

As you read about a religion, remember that within the major religions there are great differences. People are influenced by local beliefs (for example Taoism, Confucianism and Shinto in China and Japan), or by older beliefs (for example the influence of primal religion in all parts of the world, including among professing Christians). The person you meet will also have their own perspective on their faith, which may contain influences from other sources.

You may find the video teaching package *Through Their Eyes* helpful as an introduction to Hinduism, Islam and Sikhism, as living faiths in Britain today. It also contains a useful introduction to the Asian communities in Britain and the issues they face. The video and study materials are available from Interserve, 325 Kennington Road, London SE11 4QH.

You then need to see what time you have, and what other books you can get access to. The important thing is to have some initial knowledge to help you with your interviews. Learning about a particular faith is a lifetime task! You are not going to be an expert before you start your interviews; indeed a humble ignorance is more useful in approaching people of another faith than a pretence at knowledge.

Your friend may be a member of a religious movement or sect, like Zoroastrianism, Baha'i, Taoism, Jainism, or some of the new religious movements. These often have connections with the major faiths, either in the past or in the present. If you have difficulty in obtaining specific reading material on these movements, read something about a related major religion. It will help with basic ways of looking at things.

COMMUNICATING

PURPOSE

This Unit will help you with general guidance on how to communicate and how to listen to others more accurately within another culture, including an introduction to language learning.

BARRIERS TO COMMUNICATION

There are many barriers to beginning and continuing friendship with people from a different culture from oneself.

The aim of cross-cultural communication is not trying to impose information. It is trying to understand and to be understood.

The first is fear and hatred that we may have grown up with. We built this wall to keep out those who do not look or live like us. To build a friendship with them we must dismantle the wall that keeps out those whom our families may have taught us to fear.

The second barrier is our fortress of ethnocentricity and egocentrism. We looked at this in Unit 2. This shows up when we think or say, "Your way is different from mine, so you must be wrong." It shows in our assumptions and prejudices towards groups of people.

There are several ways this barrier can be manifested. First we may not readily accept criticism of our own country or culture. We need to recognise that the priorities of other cultures (like stronger family ties or a more relaxed attitude towards time) might be more biblical than our own. Secondly, we frequently want to be in the superior or controlling role – we want to be teacher instead of student, giver instead of receiver. We do not like looking stupid or inept.

We need to let go of the self-centredness that drives us to feel superior and try to control those around us. Then we can begin to accept them and their differences as unfamiliar but not necessarily wrong.

The third barrier can be the locked gate of our culture, if it emphasises independence and social and geographical mobility. We may think that it's weak to lean on people or trust in people. We protect ourselves and are reluctant to give because we will get hurt when a friend moves on. Reserve is probably the most frustrating aspect for people of more open cultures, where they may come from a circle of friends who do everything together and do not think anything of asking favours of one another.

The barriers are great but God is greater still. It is almost impossible to understand how great a barrier there was between Jews and Gentiles in the first century AD. Social, religious and historical barriers are not new to Jesus. He is able and eager to help us with the barriers we face. The wall of fear and hate can be dismantled brick by brick. We can stop fighting all that is different. We can open the locked door of our independence and ability and allow ourselves to put down roots and depend on others. We can exchange our obstacles of impatience and pushiness for the straight path of patience and sensitivity. As we do so we will be beginning to communicate across culture more effectively.

Reflect prayerfully on Ephesians 2.11-22

Consider this communication diagram:

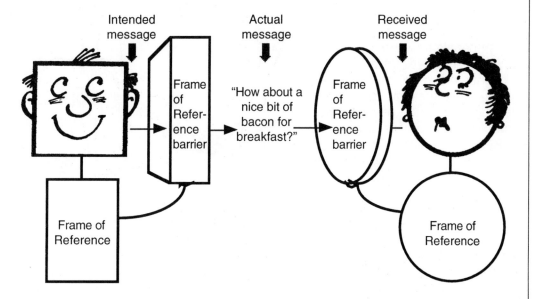

- Each person communicates out of their own frame of reference. Each person draws upon their own frame of reference for understanding the message.

- There is more to communication than just a message. There is an intended message, an actual message and a perceived message.

- Our intended message is filtered through our frame of reference and may come out in a way that differs from the intended message.

- Intended and perceived messages overlap to the extent that sender and receiver understand each other's frame of reference.

VERBAL AND NON-VERBAL

Communication is often thought of as language but it is much more than that. In all cultures non-verbal aspects are vital if communication is to be effective. We need to understand not just language, though this is important, but non-verbal cues, traits, institutions, value systems and worldviews – well enough so that mutual understanding takes place, as needed information is transmitted from one to the other effectively.

Gestures and body actions are different in different societies. So messages given may be intentional and conscious or unintentional and unconscious. Very often we use non-verbal indications without ever realising we are doing so.

British people frown when irritated, yawn when bored, smile to show recognition and acceptance, nod to agree, shake the head to say "no". But patterns of non-verbal behaviour are different in other cultures. They must be learned along with language and other aspects of the structure of the society we have entered. Otherwise we will find we communicate and perceive different messages from what were intended.

We can cause irritation, consternation or even offence to people of another culture if we use our native ways of non-verbal communicating without thinking about it.

For instance, in the small town in which I worked in India a young missionary, new to the country, came to stay. One day she went out to the post office. When she returned she was angry because two men had followed her home. After some questioning we discovered that she

had gone out without a head covering – for a woman to do this in rural India in that period indicated that she was inviting sexual advances.

Many cultures point to something they want to identify but in some societies this action is considered rude – the hand, head or lower lip may be more acceptable.

Touch behaviour is also important including striking, hitting, greeting and farewell, holding and guiding each other's movements.

> **We must discover as soon as possible what body language is appropriate in the culture we have entered. If we do not do so we may not communicate what we expect with our gestures.**

Read chapter 15. Note the suggestions there for communicating in the terms of the culture and worldview of the person with whom you are relating.

The Importance of Language

Learning a language only opens up about one tenth of all we can learn about the total way of life of its speakers. But without it we cannot communicate our personal needs, witness to the good news about Jesus, serve people with love. Even if we only expect to have a limited time in another culture it is not a waste of time to learn as much of the local language as possible.

You may think you can get by with an interpreter but this is not really adequate for anything except the superficial. Misunderstandings caused by inadequate translators run the gamut from laughable to serious mistakes causing breakdown in relationships.

Even where people use a language like English or French in discussing business or for education, they will find the local language more effective for intimate relationships. When we listen to a foreign language we are often too busy concentrating on trying to follow the vocabulary and grammar to give much attention to the underlying meaning. When we use the local language we set people free to think about the implications of the message rather than struggling to understand our speech.

Language learning also signifies that we appreciate people as people and are trying to move towards them. Also, if we are to speak about our faith it helps to emphasise that Christianity is not just a Western religion.

Our attitude is more important than what we say, but language does help us to understand people's cultural values better.

Can I do it?

Sometimes people who are going overseas to a secular job excuse themselves from language study because they feel they won't have time. This, or lack of previous experience of language learning, or age, are sometimes put forward as excuses for not learning. But plenty of determined people have proved this wrong. In language school in India I shared a teacher with someone who left school at fifteen and never learned any foreign language. She worked hard and ended up with better marks in the final examination than I did.

Thinking positively towards language learning is a crucial aspect of a learner's approach. If we do so with fear of complex sounds, structures and meanings, we hinder our learning progress. A positive approach is practical, beneficial and encouraging. Language learning can even be fun. If we earnestly want to learn, then whether young or old, with or without a formal programme of study, we can learn.

> **Motivation and need are the key factors for good language learning. People with a low aptitude can learn if they are motivated.**

People with a high aptitude fail if they are not motivated. One of the best aids to language learning is for the learner to become identified with the indigenous people. Some expatriates move on the margin of the local community. They thus reduce their opportunities to practise the language they are learning. If local people feel at ease with us in the way we relate to them they will do all in their power to assist us in speaking their language.

Being an Insider

Language is not just academic study but social activity. One of the best ways to learn both culture and language is to live for a period of several weeks with a family. Then we become an "insider". If we live apart in an expatriate environment the host community will assume that we are not really very interested in relating to them. When we then ask for help we may receive a negative response.

How do verbal and non-verbal cues relate to trust?

Millions of people all over the world speak two, three, or more languages.

LEARN THAT LANGUAGE!

David Bendor-Samuel and John Hollman

When Jesus became a man, he did not retreat behind a heavenly palisade every evening so as to appear refreshed next morning. He became one of the people. Today, it is important for a Christian worker overseas, like Christ, to become one of the people; and one of the crucial ways is through learning their language. Without it you will not be able to communicate your own personal needs, let alone communicate the good news that Jesus became a man to save people. Without learning the language of the people you will not be able to serve them with the love and sacrifice of Jesus Christ.

Even if you expect to be serving abroad for only a limited period, it is not a waste of time to try to learn the local language. There are some very good reasons why you should give time to language learning, however short you expect your stay abroad to be. Although many people can speak some English, it remains true that to be really effective in talking about spiritual things we must speak the heart language of our hearers. The English they know may be sufficient for business purposes, but that is not the language they use for intimate matters which affect beliefs and attitudes. We want them to be free to think about the implications of our message, not struggling to understand it.

Learning another person's language says some very important things about your attitude to that person and their culture. It shows appreciation of his value, of her value, as a person. It demonstrates that you are moving toward others, not demanding that they move toward you. It emphasises that the gospel is not just a 'Western' religion, but can be given expression in any language. In a short stay, your attitudes will be of much greater significance than what you say or even what you do. So the fact that you tried to speak the language will count for a great deal. Through your relationships with people outside the strict confines of your job, you will also be able to understand their cultural values much better as you seek to witness.

There are five possible ways to learn:

1. Learning by the book

Buy or borrow a book 'Teach Yourself Whatever'. Set aside weeks or months; hang a 'Don't Disturb' notice on your door; wrap a towel round your head (wet or dry according to climate) and work through the book doing all the exercises.

There are certain advantages to this solution, and many people have used it. Books are relatively cheap and you may be able to start tomorrow. You can study independently of other people, and your incompetence in the language will not embarrass anybody — especially you. But there are also disadvantages. You may not be able to find any book on the language you need, perhaps because no one has ever written one. If you do find one it may not be for the dialect that you actually need; Arabic as spoken in Egypt, for example, is quite different from Arabic spoken in Syria or in the north of Sudan, and each of these is different from Arabic spoken in the south of Sudan.

Books, by their very nature, will tend to emphasise the written form of the language rather than the spoken form, and you will not be able to get the right pronunciation from a book alone. Studying independently will encourage you to dissociate language from culture and may prevent you ever speaking the language properly.

2. Learning on a course

Enrol for a course designed to teach you the target language, attend it regularly and practise between classes. The course may be in your home country, or in the country where you expect to serve, or in any country where the language is spoken as the main language (e.g. learn French in France).

You will have the discipline of the class schedule to keep you at it, with other students to encourage you. You may have opportunity for oral practice. However, you may not be able to keep up the pace of the rest of the class, or you may become bored because they are too slow. You may be too unsure of yourself or your language ability to participate in the oral class activities. You may be dependent upon the language as known by the teacher, who may be a foreigner to the language, or speak a dialect other than the one you want to learn. Unless it is recommended to you by somebody who knows the course and knows you and your needs, you may have little idea of the scope and quality of the course before you start.

3. Learning by immersion

Go out to where you will be working; live with a family who speak only the language you want to learn. Then find somebody outside of that family who will help you with the language. Work with this person one or two hours each day and practise with the family and with anybody else you can find for the rest of the time.

With this approach you will learn the dialect and variety of the language that you actually need; you will focus on oral rather than written language, and you will be using the language to communicate from the very beginning. You will, in fact, learn more than the language — you will learn how people live and think. You are likely to make friends who will remain friends for the rest of your life. You may have great opportunities to share your knowledge of Jesus with the family and great opportunity to learn dependence upon the Lord.

That may sound great, but you will feel lost for words in many situations, although if you do not allow yourself to withdraw you will eventually find the right words. You could also be overwhelmed by the amount of language you are being exposed to. And it may be difficult to find a family willing to take you into their home and put up with your 'stupidity' — even the young children will speak better than you at first.

4. Learning by immersion with a life jacket

Attend a course, such as those given by the Summer Institute of Linguistics, to learn how to learn a language; then once you have finished the course, continue with solution 3 above. For many people, this is probably the best method (with a book to help you as well).

At such a course you will learn something of how languages are structured and what to expect in a foreign language – you will then be less likely to sink under the sheer volume of the language as you first encounter it. You will be taught techniques for learning the different aspects of any language. You will learn how to make a whole range of exotic sounds which will prepare you for practically any language. If you do not understand the system used by the people for writing their own language, you will have learned how to write down new words using phonetic symbols; this is especially helpful when the language is not written down at all. You will be working with others in similar situations to yourself, many of whom were not good at languages at school but who will go on to master complex languages all over the world.

On such a course, however, you will probably not learn one word of the language that you want to learn! Rather, you will learn how to learn. To attend the course will take six weeks of your valuable time before going overseas – six weeks which will prepare you for a lifetime of language learning. And it will cost some money. But it is an investment which will pay rich dividends.

5. Learning by analysis

For those whose major contribution overseas is going to be in the area of language there is yet one more option to consider: attend courses over a nine-month period at the Summer Institute of Linguistics to learn how to analyse a previously unwritten language. Then devote the next few years to living among the people, learning their language really well and writing it down. You would then be equipped to go to literacy work, Bible translation or other language-related service.

The advantages are the same as for solution 4, but the preparation is more thorough and you will gain skills beyond those learned in the six-week course. Your opportunity to contribute something worthwhile to the people will be greatly increased; you could be giving them the Word of God in their own language. But it takes time. In fact it takes your life – not necessarily

WELL RODNEY..... THERE'S A COUPLE OF NEW WORDS FOR YOU TO PRACTICE!

your whole life-time, but a total involvement for the years that it takes. It actually takes a specific call of God.

Problems you will encounter

Language learning is not easily achieved; most of us must expect to face some difficulties. Chief among them may well be slow progress; you feel you will never be able to talk freely! That is just a fact you will have to learn to live with; after all, you did not make much progress with English during your first two years of trying! To keep on trying is the important thing, and to add a little more each day. Therefore you will need to set your priorities carefully and impose a little self-discipline, lest the natural desire to spend time on things which seem to give quick results distracts you.

As all the books and courses will tell you, learning a second language is primarily a question of acquiring a new set of habits and reactions – something like learning to drive a car! Learning things by heart still has a place, but careful listening and a willingness to mimic and be laughed at are as important as memory drills, and much more fun. More than anything else, your progress will be the out-working of your attitudes to the new language and the people who speak it – which is why you need to start to learn even if you are only staying there a month or two.

You must expect to find some unfamiliar sounds which you will master before long, just as every child does – provided, that is, that you are willing to keep on being corrected (and can find friends willing to help you). Differences in the sounds will probably include some strange consonants or vowels and

perhaps the more subtle differences of tone (syllables being pronounced at different pitch levels to give a different meaning) and of intonation (the tune of the sentence as a whole).

Then there will be differences of grammatical pattern – the way the parts of sentences are put together. You can expect to find a different order of words, such as 'kill man tiger lake by will plural' (the man will kill tigers by the lake). There may be affixes or inflections added to all the words in a phrase (he bought two-a little-a black-a kittens-a) or unexpected ways of saying things (I go come).

You will want to learn a few new words of vocabulary each day, especially at first. Concentrate on words that you will be able to use in your life situation, for using words helps you remember them. You will also want to learn by heart useful phrases such as greetings, questions, imperatives, conversation openers and sustainers (these give the impression you have understood!). So do set yourself up with lists of things to learn and do use the words as you learn them. A few at a time, and put to use straight away, is the way to beat memory fatigue.

Above all, do remember that languages are learned as people try to speak them! So don't give up, all embarrassed, when you make a mistake. In the short term, it is not the progress you make that counts so much as whether or not you make the attempt. The Lord is able to bless your efforts far beyond what they merit in this as in everything else.

LEARNING METHODS

COURSES AVAILABLE

The Summer Institute of Linguistics six-week language-learning course is held near High Wycombe, Buckinghamshire, starting early July every year. Similar courses are held in France and Germany. For details write to SIL, Horsleys Green, High Wycombe, Bucks HP14 3XL.

It is unlikely that people going to another culture into secular work will be able to set aside a period of months or even weeks for language learning but nevertheless they can do something. The suggestions which follow are adapted from the LAMP method devised by Thomas and Elizabeth Brewster. This method enables one to study a language step by step without the benefit of formal language studies. Learners make friends in the local community and find a language helper. Friendships are established and the learner learns and practises some of the new language daily.

Practice

Practice is essential when learning a language. It is always preferable to listen to a person for whom the language is their mother tongue rather an expatriate, however fluent they may be. Hearing alone is not enough. That must come first. But if it is not followed up with plenty of speaking practice, progress will be slow. Some learners hesitate to jump in and start using the language in case they make mistakes. But one has to do this in order to learn. Reading, learning grammatical rules and lists of vocabulary are no use unless they are put into frequent use in conversation.

"Languages must be learned if Christ is to be communicated in the words of men, for this cannot be done outside of the total framework of a culture of which the language is an integral part. Let's take time to be good language learners. If we truly do, God will enable us to be better communicators for Him." (Eugene Nida)

Mimicry

Mimicry is the key to language learning. It consists of two phases:
- Careful listening and observing
- Constant practice

Observation

Observation as we listen is important. We note whether the mouth is open or mostly closed, or what other movement of the lips, tongue and teeth are used. Some sounds will be entirely new and will have to be practised frequently.

Not only words, phrases and sentences in the new language must be learned, but also the structure of conversation. For example some African cultures do not use the question-answer sequence. For them information is precious and should not easily be given away.

Many cultures run on a period of informal chat before people get down to business. In some cases this lasts about half-an-hour. In some Asian countries "no" is rarely used; "yes" can mean "no" or "perhaps". To say "no" would be too direct.

All Work and No Play?

Language study is not all work. As we progress in the language we become fascinated that people understand us when we speak. The more one speaks the language, mixes with local people and engages them in conversation the faster one will learn. In the process the ability to speak will increase and this achievement will bring a certain amount of satisfaction and personal enrichment. In particular we will have the joy and satisfaction of being able to share God's love, sometimes with people who know nothing about it.

Children seem to make a game of learning language. Their early attempts are seldom "correct" from an adult standpoint but the child is not self-conscious about his "mistakes" and usually receives much positive reinforcement from his efforts. Besides repeating sounds, words and phrases over and over, they experiment with different ways of saying the same thing. They seem to talk just for the pleasure of hearing themselves. When they learn question forms they seem to ask questions just for the joy of getting responses (it often drives their parents to distraction). A child's fascination with language and his lack of self-consciousness are his greatest assets in acquiring a language. These assets motivate him to practise using what he knows in a natural unforced manner.
(World Mission, Vol. 3: *The Cultural Dimension*, page 64)

From this brief description of how a child learns language, what do you anticipate might inhibit an adult language learner?

What benefits do you see in communicating what little you know immediately rather than waiting until you reach a higher level of competency?

G
Get what you need.

L
Learn what you get.

U
Use what you learn.

E
Evaluate.

The GLUE method is based on the LAMP approach pioneered by Thomas and Elizabeth Brewster. This approach offers an invaluable means of establishing an acceptable role in the host community. The full course is called *Language Acquisition Made Practical: Field methods for language learners*, by E. Thomas Brewster and Elizabeth S. Brewster (Colorado Springs: Lingua House, 1976). The course provides excellent opportunities for bonding to occur and for acculturation and identification to blossom. Its emphasis on communication allows ministry to take place during the language learning process, not at a far off date when a degree of proficiency is attained.

The objective is to improve and refine your techniques and to adapt your attitude to maximise efficient language learning.

G Get what you need.

If you are to communicate you will need to be able to say something to those you contact. As you start, you will depend heavily on memorised texts. To learn these texts you will need to find a native speaker of the target language who has some understanding of the language you speak as well. You will also need a notebook so that you can note down all those things you want to memorise. A tape recorder, if possible, is also a help to record what your helper says so that he does not have to repeat it so many times.

Remember, you are in charge. You explain to your helper what you want to say. If you really want to learn it, or feel that you must learn it the chances are better that you will plan to learn it.

L Learn what you get.

Explain to your helper how you want to learn it. Suggested sequence is: listen, mimic, practice.

Listen.
Ask your language helper to say the text several times at normal speed so that you can listen to it. Have him do the action as he says it; record it if possible.

Mimic.
Ask your helper to say and do it first and then you repeat and do it after him. Pay close attention to pronunciation and intonation and the music and rhythm of the language. Make sure your helper corrects your mistakes. An effective sequence is:

- phrase drill – break each sentence into small phrases and then mimic each phrase three times. Go through it again doing each phrase once. Be sure to incorporate the actions where appropriate.

- build up drill – start again with the phrases and build up so that you can mimic the whole sentence. Start either with the last or first

U Use what you learn.

You must take the initiative to go out and practise what you are learning. This is often the most difficult part for many language learners.

From the first day you should be using what you learn to practise communicating and interacting with people. Without this vital element language learning will be reduced to an exercise in memorisation.

E Evaluate.

You must look objectively at yourself to see how you are doing. Here are some suggestions:

- Reflect on the progress you are making. Encourage yourself!
- Look at your motivation and your morale. Any bolstering necessary?
- What are you having problems with? Any ideas for solutions?

Here are some example phrases you might try to learn:

- Hello. My name is _____. What is your name?
- I have lost my way. Can you help me?
- I am very tired and hungry.
- It is a pleasure to be in your country.
- I have just begun to learn your language.
- Thank you for helping me today.

Once you obtain the text from your helper check its suitability. Can it be used with everyone regardless of age, sex or position? Does it sound natural? Next, transcribe the text into your notebook or have your helper do it. Then, try to understand the meaning of each phrase you have written. Write the meaning down in your notebook. You will also want to note problems and opportunities in your text. The first problems will probably be difficulties of pronunciation. You should also note opportunities the text presents to expand your knowledge of the language. Finally you want to record the text on a tape recorder. Your helper should repeat each phrase of the text several times, leaving a pause (for you to say it in practice) between each repetition.

phrase of each sentence, and work up to saying the whole sentence. Incorporate the actions where appropriate.

- sentence drill – mimic the sentences and the actions three times each. Go straight through it again one time each.

Practice

Ask your helper to follow this sequence:

- completion drill – go through the whole text, have your helper say all but the last couple of words of each sentence. You say the whole sentence with action each time. Go through the text several times this way, having your helper leave off more and more words each time, until you are able to say and do all the sentences without any prompting. Have your helper say and do the whole sentence after you each time, to be sure you get it right.

- alternation drill – if your text is a dialogue, have your helper take one role and you take the other. Reverse roles and go through it again. Incorporate the actions.

- practice alone – this is where a tape recording of the text can be valuable. Practise with the tape, repeating the phrases you recorded from your helper. When you can reproduce the text without stumbling or hesitation you will have achieved the degree of fluency you need to go further.

Effective communication is your goal and you begin your tentative steps towards achieving it the first day of language learning. Here are some suggestions:

- Make a habit of being friendly with people.
- Try to find some people who are always there – office receptionist, office colleague, neighbour, shopkeeper, street vendor, shoe-shine boy, newsstand attendant.
- Get to know them and establish yourself as a friend and as a learner with them.
- Practise what you are learning on them.
- Tell them you would like to come back and practise with them on a regular basis.

- Look at each part of your method looking for your strengths and weaknesses, reactions and attitudes.
- Think of some ideas of how to help yourself make more contacts with people.
- Think about what you want to learn next.
- Organise your material. Keep your notes and cultural observations organised and up-to-date so that you have ready access to all accumulated information.

Your daily evaluation allows you to measure your language learning effectiveness and make appropriate adjustments. It keeps you organised from day to day, allowing you to set realistic goals and work on specific areas of weakness. It also provides a record of your experiences, attitudes and personal progress.

PERSONAL REFLECTION

FURTHER READING

E T And E S Brewster, *LAMP
(Language Acquisition Made
Practical): Field Methods for
Language Learners,* Published
1976 by Lingua House, 915 West
Jackson, Colorado Springs,
Colorado 80907, USA. Very clear,
practical and easy to use.

E T and E S Brewster, *LEARN!
Language Exploration and
Acquisition Resource Notebook,*
Lingua House, 1981. Address as
above.

D N Larson and W A Smalley,
*Becoming Bilingual — a Guide to
Language Learning.* Published
1972 and available from William
Carey Library, 533 Hermosa
Street, South Pasadena, California
91030, USA. An excellent and
practical volume, but rather more
technical than LAMP.

E W Stevick, *Teaching and Learning
Languages,* Cambridge University
Press 1982.

H Douglas Brown, *Principles of
Language Learning and Teaching,*
Prentice-Hall 1980

A Healey (ed), *Language Learner's
Field Guide,* Summer Institute of
Linguistics 1975.

D N Larson, *Guidelines for Barefoot
Language Learning. An Approach
through Involvement and
Independence.* Published 1984 by
CMS Publishing Inc, 3570 North
Rice Street, St Paul, Minnesota
55112, USA

What groups or kinds of people
do you fear or dislike
(see page 80)?

When was the last time
you were in a "learner"
rather than a "teacher" role?

Do you tend to be too
frightened to speak about Jesus?
Or too pushy in telling people
about him?

Think of some
examples of situations you
have been in where the intended
and perceived messages were
different? How could you have
avoided the problems that
arose?

TENSIONS
AND
DIFFICULTIES

PURPOSE

This Unit will help you to get the measure of some of the particular difficulties faced by living in another culture, in the light of the kind of person you are.

CROSS-CULTURAL LIVING

Often in our cultural arrogance we disapprove of what we perceive as the weaknesses of other cultures. In doing this we create a wall of rejection and hinder the work of Christ. But if we are truly His servants, we shall seek to serve Him and the people of the culture we have entered. We have been trying to learn how to do this in the previous Units – through acceptance and trust, learning social skills, and learning to communicate.

The key to successful personal relationships in our new culture is to understand and accept others as having a viewpoint as worthy of existence as our own.

We have seen above all the importance of friendship. When we have friends in our new culture, they will open many doors for us.

But this does not all happen easily. It can produce emotional strain. Changing the patterns of thinking and living of a lifetime does not happen overnight. However open and friendly we may be, there will be areas where our culture has very different perceptions. If we do not understand these differences they can cause enormous frustration and tension. Even when we do understand them, it is still hard to adjust to them.

Lingenfelter and Mayers in their book *Ministering Cross-Culturally* identified a number of key areas which different cultures perceive very differently. We shall look at these more closely in this Unit.

MINISTERING CROSS-CULTURALLY

by

Lingenfelter and Mayers

<u>CONTENTS</u>

* how people use time

* how people make judgments

* how people handle crises

* what people consider worthwhile goals

* what the basis of people's self worth is

* what people's attitudes are to vulnerability

TIME

The concept of being late varies significantly from culture to culture. This is because some cultures are time oriented, others are event oriented. Both orientations are valid but some people are happier with no set routine whereas others are more comfortable with a precise schedule.

In general Western culture is time oriented and several non-Western cultures are event oriented. We can easily label the latter as time wasters. But they can feel that "time" cultures are uncaring because they are more concerned with time than the significance of an event.

In event oriented cultures church services rarely begin on time. But neither are people in a hurry to finish at a particular time. Once they have arrived and the event is under way, they become involved in it. People are often late for time structured meetings because the activities they were previously involved in did not finish on time. Time oriented people are soon weary of discussions and call for a vote, whereas event oriented people want to consider the problem exhaustively, hear everybody's views and deliberate until there is a unanimous agreement. History in general is more important than exact dates. For example in some cultures many people have no idea of their date of birth but know its chronological order in relation to other events.

Time oriented people will work at a single project until it is completed. Event oriented people may do a bit here and there on different tasks. For example, a shop assistant may attend to some of your needs and then attend to someone else before completing your order. The different attitudes will also show in things like walking pace. Time oriented people are determined to reach the place they are aiming for as quickly as possible. To them event oriented people seem merely to stroll everywhere.

If you are a time oriented person you will feel frustrated in an event oriented culture. Try to go to event oriented activities at your convenience rather than at the stated time given.

JUDGMENT

Some cultures systemise and sort information they receive and fit it into a particular structure. Each problem is distinct and separate and can be reduced to right and wrong options. Detail is sorted on the basis of a perceived order. Such people often enjoy crossword puzzles or biblical word studies. Other cultures do not separate particulars from the context of the larger picture. For them the whole is greater than the parts. They may enjoy chess, or prefer to learn things by participation, for example by being an apprentice.

Some people think in terms of right or wrong, and failure can destroy a life of service. Others are open-ended in their attitude. They consider all persons flawed, therefore failure is not seen as the end of a person's usefulness in a particular place of service. They consider most areas grey and open to debate. They are uncomfortable with standardised proceedings and rigidly applied rules. In particularised cultures teachers are judged on how well they teach, not on their treatment of their family. In a generalised culture people will withhold judgment on this point until they find out something about that teacher as a whole person.

Such a culture may be accused of softness, lack of principle and inconsistency. But we can create great difficulty by insisting that others think and judge in the same way as we do. As Christians we need to learn to accept others in love, not to try and make them into our image. One of the principles of incarnation is to learn to think in the style of the culture we have adopted.

CRISES

Some cultures are crisis oriented while others are non-crisis oriented. The former look ahead to potential problems. Non-crisis oriented people may be familiar with precautionary procedures but ignore them. They don't worry. They play down the likelihood of a crisis and avoid taking action for as long as possible. When a crisis actually happens they derive a solution from whatever alternatives they perceive in the situation. Usually they react to crises with a sense of humour. When I was in Jamaica shortly after the destructive hurricane Gilbert in the autumn of 1988 I was constantly entertained with jokes about the hurricane. Top of the Pops in Jamaica for the year was a humorous song about it. Such people are often sceptical of experts and see themselves as qualified by their experience to handle the problem.

Crisis oriented people plan growth and change years ahead. Individuals not capable of working with the plan may be bypassed, overruled or dismissed. It is a common error for such people to assume that others understand them when they have heard their words. They often feel that their way of handling crises is the best. But if we want to build up mutual understanding we must cooperate with people who think differently, to make decisions which benefit the whole community.

GOALS

Some cultures tend to be task oriented whereas others tend to be people oriented. Task oriented people gain their satisfaction in reaching their objectives and completing projects. They may consider too many social activities a waste of time and prefer to work uninterrupted. They are able to endure social deprivation to reach their goal.

People oriented individuals find their satisfaction in relationships with others and give a higher priority to maintaining these. They need the acceptance of a group of associates and spend significant amounts of time and energy fulfilling obligations to the group. They will sacrifice their personal interests for those of others.

Task oriented people may be intolerant of those people less committed than themselves to the job in hand. They may choose the most productive workers as leaders but discover later that they are not gifted in personal relationships.

People oriented individuals are often not going to sacrifice interpersonal relationships for long hours of study and end up with a poor academic record. But this may not be a reliable indicator of their ability to make good on a job. Christians who are task oriented want to lead people to Christ, but often push this to the margin of their activities because they are busy trying to finish their "work". We need to be more open to respect other people and share our lives (including priorities and goals) with those to whom we want to minister.

SELF-WORTH

Some cultures are achievement focused, whereas many other people are status focused. The latter count family background and social position as more important than personal accomplishments. They believe a person's character closely resembles that of their parents and most individuals derive their self worth from the prestige ascribed to their position in life. Titles such as Doctor and Reverend are highly valued. Degrees after one's name, even "failed BA", also give prestige.

Status-focused prestige tends to be permanent whereas for achievement-focused people it is temporary. An athlete will be praised for his recent performances but forgotten when superseded by others. Achievers often develop a very critical attitude towards others. Those who are less gifted may develop envy and low self-esteem.

Cross-cultural workers must be aware of their own concept of the basis of personal identity and self-worth. Then they must determine the attitude of their adopted culture.

We need to recognise that a needs for prestige, in whatever way it is sought, will run contrary to the role of servanthood to which God calls His followers. But we have to acknowledge the cultural standards of those around. Servanthood requires that we subject ourselves to the authority of the social norm in which we find ourselves. We need to live a life consistent with the self worth we have in God while being sensitive to the feelings of others.

VULNERABILITY

Some cultures try to conceal their vulnerability, others expose it. The former try to avoid failure and error at all costs. They would rather not run in a race than appear inept, prefer not to take an examination rather than fail. If they make mistakes they will try hard to cover up or excuse them. A teacher makes a mistake if she publicly praises a student in a culture where vulnerability is concealed. Her action is seen as severe criticism of the others. Such a student may purposefully fail for weeks to come rather than expose the shortcomings of the rest of the class. Anything new or unusual is suspect because it is not part of their experience and is thus open to uncertainty. They may not like to enter a new situation or take part in an unfamiliar activity because it does not allow them to control their performance.

Those who like to expose vulnerability are willing to risk failure. They consider it important to finish a race and endure to the bitter end, whatever the outcome. They regularly entertain views other than their own and are open to the criticism and suggestions of others.

If those who are ready to expose their vulnerability expose the errors of those who do the reverse, they can cause great anxiety and their behaviour will be seen as cruel and hurtful. They must realise that "losing face" is a terrible thing in the eyes of people who like to conceal their vulnerability. For example in some cultures it is usual to talk directly to an employee whose work is unsatisfactory. In other cultures it is more acceptable to use a go-between to talk to them. The former will think this cowardly but the latter will be pleased that they have not been exposed.

ARE YOU LIKE THIS?

Read carefully the situations described overleaf. On the line below each situation indicate by a cross your reaction to the situation, in keeping with what you like, feel, sense about yourself – that this is the way you do act, think, behave. Place the cross toward the left if the situation is characteristic of you and toward the right if it is not.

Example
May and Bob attend church each week, but Bob doesn't seem to care to be on time. May gets irritated, nearly every week. Would you become irritated as May does in the same situation?

(me)_____x_____(not me)

This response indicates that you would get irritated a bit, but not too much and not always; and the irritation would not be likely to affect your relationship with Bob. A cross on the extreme left would indicate that you would always be intensely irritated by this practice and a cross on the extreme right would indicate that you would not care and are probably the same way as Bob.

When you respond, attempt to do so as much as possible in keeping with your actual felt response in the same or a similar situation. Try to think of one. Do not answer as you think you are – or (worse) as you think you ought to be or would like to be.

ARE

YOU

1. Harry thinks that a person who is not able to get to work on time is not a very satisfactory worker. Do you agree with Harry?

(me) _____ (not me)

2. Carol starts each morning by making a schedule of the day. She gets upset when something or someone interferes with it. Are you like Carol?

(me) _____ (not me)

3. Marilyn works for the Boss who likes her to stay overtime if all her work is not caught up. She resists this since she plans her time ahead and expects to do something else when she finishes work. Would you resist like Marilyn?

(me) _____ (not me)

4. Joan was listening to two speakers. One had all the facts under control and the other had actual personal experience with the problem but was not as detailed and organised in his presentation. She became engrossed in the factual presentation rather than the other. Would you have been like Joan?

(me) _____ (not me)

5. One evening Sheila had been studying for three hours while her room mate gave up after just one hour to go and talk with friends. Sheila turned to her and asked her how she would ever learn anything since she can't learn just from talks with people. "You must learn from experts in the field of what's happened in the past." Would you feel like Sheila did?

(me) _____ (not me)

6. Bill takes full and careful notes whenever he's in a meeting listening to a speaker for fear that he will overlook something that is important. Do you take notes like Bill?

(me) _____ (not me)

7. Sally keeps her home spotless. Everything has its place and everything is in place. Are you like Sally?

(me) _____ (not me)

8. Jack had to choose between two groups in which to participate. One he knew was going to be well organised and efficient, but the other would allow him room for independent thought. He finally chose the former. Would you be likely to choose the first also?

(me) _____ (not me)

9. A political speaker was definitive about things that were right and wrong. Jim agreed but Harry got uptight since he felt the man was too dogmatic. Would you be more definitive like Jim?

(me) _____ (not me)

10. Larry's neighbour likes to drop in for a visit in the evening after work, and sometimes stays to talk for a long time. Since Larry often works at home in the evening, he gets annoyed at these seemingly endless and pointless conversations which prevent him from getting his work done. Would you get annoyed like Larry?

(me) _____ (not me)

LIKE THIS?

11. Charles finds that his closest friends tend to be people whose interests and careers goals are similar to his own. Are you like Charles?

(me)_____(not me)

12. Steve will really push himself to get the mark he wants in a course even if it means going without sleep and working himself to the point of exhaustion. Are you are you a worker like Steve?

(me)_____(not me)

13. Nick is always careful to address people with their proper title such as Dr., Rev., Mr. It bothers him when other people ignore such titles. Are you like Nick?

(me)_____(not me)

14. Ken feels it a terrible shame that a friend of his did all the course work for his PhD, but never wrote the thesis because he said he didn't care about the degree. Would you feel the same way as Ken?

(me)_____(not me)

15. Peter is bothered by the fact that some of the younger faculty members on his campus never wear coats and ties. He says he can never tell them from the students. Would your reaction be like Peter's?

(me)_____(not me)

16. Paul enjoys a good argument and will often go on talking at some length to prove his point, even if it is relatively insignificant. Are you likely to argue like Paul.

(me)_____(not me)

17. On a trip to visit some relatives in the city, Dave inadvertently took a wrong turn. When his wife Sally asked if they were on the right road Dave explained he was looking for a short cut. Would you have covered up your mistake as Dave did?

(me)_____(not me)

18. When David and Sally finally arrived at their relatives' home, Sally immediately began to tell them about how they had got lost on the way. Dave felt this was entirely unnecessary and was rather upset with Sally. Would you have been upset with Sally?

(me)_____(not me)

19. Ruth's Bible study leader always asked very personal questions, and tried to get people to open up and "let it all hang out". This bothered Ruth and she usually gave rather vague answers to the personal questions. Would you react like Ruth?

(me)_____(not me)

20. Diane feels that it is usually best to try to work out personal problems on your own rather than going to a friend for help. Do you agree with Diane?

(me)_____(not me)

Read chapter 13 which outlines a
Biblical worldview.

Whether you realise it or not, your culture will have influenced your answers
to all of those questions. But within the same culture we each have our own
personality differences, for example in our attitude to time and events. This
varies greatly from person to person.

This exercise has helped you to analyse your own attitude to the areas we
have been exploring in this Unit. Spend a few minutes reflecting on your
answers, and what they might indicate about you and your culture. Are there
aspects of yourself which you realise you would have extreme difficulty in
changing, if you wanted to do so in response to a new culture?

Write some reflections here.

And we must not forget the spiritual dimension...

SPIRITUAL WARFARE

Ruth Giesner

Two groups of Christian workers in Africa disagreed over a plan of action. They became critical of each other and harsh words were spoken. A visiting leader was told about this by one group, and as he prayed he felt sure this was a spiritual attack. So he called the group to pray that God would defeat Satan and expose his lies and blindness. Within three days an apology came from the other group. 'We can see things clearly now and don't know why we were so negative,' they said.

Right through the Bible we read of spiritual warfare. Satan continually opposes God and tries to block his plans to give eternal life to all people. This battle reaches its climax in the gospels as Satan repeatedly tries to destroy Christ. He seems to win a great victory when Christ is crucified, but the willing, physical death of the eternal Son of God is not defeat. It is in fact the greatest victory because as his sinless life-blood is shed, atonement is made for our sin, God's law is satisfied, and forgiveness for sin is freely offered to all humanity (Leviticus 17:11, Ephesians 1:7). So the sin and death sequence is smashed and Satan's power over us is broken. Satan goes on trying to deceive

the world, and he has his helpers, but his efforts are doomed. The fact is, Christ has conquered Satan: 'Having disarmed the powers and authorities, he made a public spectacle of them, triumphing over them by the cross' (Colossians 2:15).

So there is nothing new or unusual about spiritual warfare. The Christian is part of a very big campaign; the crucial battle has been won already, victory is secure and there are adequate instructions and resources for our protection and advance. But because of Satan's tactics, Christians are constantly in warfare against him and his allies. 'Our

struggle is... against the authorities, against the powers of this dark world and against the spiritual forces of evil in the heavenly realms. Therefore put on the full armour of God... stand your ground... and pray in the Spirit on all occasions' (Ephesians 6:10-18).

No one goes into a major warfare on his own. He is always part of a big campaign, although sometimes he may feel alone or face a single opponent. In warfare each person has a vital part to play for which he is given orders and equipment. He also needs to know who the enemy is and what the battle is about. That is as true for us as we embark on any form of Christian service as it is for a military person.

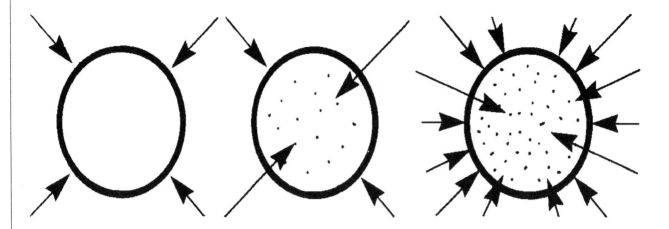

Recognise the signs of attack

In the physical germ warfare waged by our bodies, we are constantly being attacked and surrounded by germs, yet we are not often aware of them. But if our defences are weakened, we show signs of illness.

Similarly, in spiritual warfare we have our normal God-given protection (which I outline later), but if this is weakened for any reason, or if we are in a place of strong spiritual attack, we will become more aware of the warfare and will need to know how to resist and combat these forms of attack. We also need each others' help, care and prayer.

There are two kinds of 'symptoms' of spiritual attack:

1. Personal and within ourselves.
In our Christian life we may find we start doubting God's presence or the power of the Christian message. We may neglect listening to God, praying, and having fellowship with others. We may fall into lower standards of Christian living, or into negativity which leads to discouragement and despair. Finally, we may forget that the Holy Spirit is our constant companion and help.

2. Corporate and from outside.
In our Christian service we may discover resistance to the message which makes us discouraged. Rejection by local people may produce dismay, and their misunderstanding of our motives may produce anger. There could also be misunderstandings within the team which break down fellowship. Opposition by those of other faiths can make us fearful. We may become conscious of spiritual oppression and wonder if it is worth going on. We may also be subject to direct spiritual attack, even including curses or the use of occult powers

against us.

All these signs may be 'the flaming arrows of the evil one' (Ephesians 6:16), and we need to remember how Jesus recognised Satan in the wilderness temptations and how he dealt with them.

Recognise the enemy

Before studying anything to do with Satan, we should always focus on our Lord Jesus Christ who came 'to destroy the devil's work' (1 John 3:8). Over every activity of Satan we can write, 'Jesus has power and authority to destroy this work.' Praise Jesus, worship him and ask him specifically to destroy Satan's work whenever you encounter it. A good example of this is in Acts 4:23-31.

Satan has many names in scripture, and these reflect his activities. He is 'the god of this age/world'. He stops people coming to faith in Jesus by 'blinding the minds of unbelievers' (2 Corinthians 4:4). They literally cannot take in what we say. He is also the ruler of the kingdom of the air, and as such is 'the spirit who is now at work in those who are disobedient' (Ephesians 2:2). He actively prevents them from turning to Christ.

The name Satan means adversary, accuser. He accuses Christians to God, as he did Job (Job 1:9). He was wrong! He accuses Christians to themselves, making them feel unworthy and rejected, not righteous (Revelation 12:10). He accuses Christians to one another especially in the church. His lies and deceptions can divide us and cause us to exaggerate faults and differences. Satan accuses Christians to the world by distorting their teaching, causing caricatures to be drawn of them, drawing people's attention to our failures, and so on (Matthew 5:11).

Satan can cause physical illness and harm, too, as with Job (Job 2:7) and the woman who was bent over (Luke 13:16). For example, a Christian worker was cursed by evil, antagonistic men and before long his son was found to have cancer. This particular cancer was completely removed by specific prayer to break the curse and free the whole family from its effects.

Satan also destroys life. Violence, murder and suicide are often the results of his deception as people are drawn into drugs, alcohol and occult practices (John 8:44).
The term 'the devil' means tempter, slanderer. He tempts Christians to sin and diverts them from believing God's Word, as he did with Eve and with Jesus.

He also leads Christians into extreme doctrine and heresy (2 Timothy 2:26), and inspires false teaching. This can include cults and ideologies which may look good to people, such as the Spiritualist Church, but the power in them is satanic (1 Timothy 4:1; Revelation 3:9). He hinders the work of the church, even stirring up opposition and persecution (Revelation 2:9ff).

As Beelzebub, the prince of demons (Luke 11:14-26), Satan causes demonic oppression and possession. There are many examples of this in scripture, notably the Gadarene man (Luke 8:29), an incident which also demonstrates the complete authority of Jesus over demons.

The hidden power of the occult

In Saudi Arabia I was once the guest for dinner of a Christian couple and their two small children. They had lived in Riyadh, the capital, for several years and had all kept fit and well. A few months before my visit they had moved to their present house and had all been sick off and on. The little girl was especially unwell. My host and hostess asked me what I thought about the situation. I replied that the sickness could be due to natural causes like a contaminated water supply or that it might have a satanic origin due to evil powers inhabiting the house. At this one of the other guests laughed and I knew that I could not proceed to explain more. I promised to pray for the family.

I shared the problem with the couple with whom I was staying and we specifically prayed for healing and for the Lord's victory to be evident. Unexpectedly I visited the home the next day. The scoffer was not present. The little girl was still ill. I suggested to the parents and the three other visitors that we should join together as a team and pray for cleansing in each room of the house. Accordingly we went from room to room and prayed for the casting out of evil and for cleansing through the blood of Christ. We then praised God and prayed for those who used the particular room and for its special uses. For example, in the kitchen we prayed for the one who cooked, and for those who ate the food.

A Muslim neighbour visited the house a few hours after this service had taken place. She exclaimed in astonishment: 'Your little girl is now well and your home has a different atmosphere. What has happened?' The lady of the house told her of the power of Jesus Christ and how a group of believers had prayed in his name and that all evil had been expelled. This proved an effective and convincing way to share with her the good news of Jesus' victory over sin and evil.

God is constantly warning his people of Satan's power and activities and telling us not to get involved with supernatural power which is not his power but Satan's. Deuteronomy 18:9-12 lists occult practices forbidden to God's people. These are common today under a wide range of names and it is important that we know what they are and teach young Christians to renounce them.

Divination is discovering hidden knowledge by using satanic power such as clairvoyance, astrology, horoscopes and ouija boards (Acts 16:16-19).

Sorcery is fortune-telling by interpreting dreams, visions, reading palms and head bumps.

Interpreting omens means foretelling events by reading signs such as the flight of birds, entrails of animals and tea-leaves in cups.

GOD Creator, Father	CHRIST All-powerful, victorious	HOLY SPIRIT The enabler

KINGDOM OF SATAN
DARKNESS
SIN
DEATH

KINGDOM OF GOD
LIGHT
RIGHTEOUSNESS
LIFE

SATAN
Prince of this world,
a created being

ANGELS
Ministering spirits

FALLEN ANGELS
Demons who do his work

SONS OF THE KINGDOM
People who receive and use
God's authority

SONS OF THE EVIL ONE
People who receive and use
Satan's authority

Witchcraft is the use of magic, manipulating spirits to control people, casting spells, and using drugs and potions to induce certain actions or conditions of mind. Any form of bewitching, enchanting, spells, curses and incantations invoking the power of evil spirits over people or animals falls into this category.

Mediums are controlled by evil spirits and become a channel for communicating with demons who impersonate the dead and give false information (Leviticus 20:3-25).

In addition to the normal beliefs and practices in most religions, there are also superstitions and occult activities. These are most obvious at times of crisis, particularly illness or disaster, when people go to mediums, shamans, witch-doctors, etc. In Hinduism, transcendental meditation and Yoga are stated ways of contacting the power of Hindu gods and applying this to yourself. In Islam there is fear and belief in Djinn (spirits), 'evil eye', 'hand of Fatima', etc. The Zikkas and the practices of Dervishes directly invoke occult power, inducing trances and supernatural phenomena. In much traditional religion there is open demonstration of demonic possession and the manipulating of spirits. Many ceremonies performed in other faiths fascinate Christian workers. It is important to realise that sometimes demonic powers are

being invoked and to be near them can make us vulnerable to spiritual oppression.

How to win the battles
There are six steps which we should take in order to experience the Lord's victory in our lives and service.

1. Know your weaknesses
If you have unconfessed sin, this will weaken you and your witness, and invite Satan's accusations. Share the problem with someone and claim God's forgiveness and victory. If we refuse to forgive others, we will cause broken relationships. Paul speaks of this in 2 Corinthians 2:5-11: 'I have forgiven in the sight of Christ for your sake, in order that Satan might not outwit us. For we are not unaware of his schemes.' If you have been involved with any cult, heresy or occult practice, renounce it, receive God's cleansing and forgiveness, and ask someone to pray that the power of it may be broken in Jesus' name. It is possible that parents' actions in drug taking, immorality, and occult practices (particularly Spiritism) can harm the next generations (Numbers 14:18; Leviticus 26:39-42), and if we are oppressed spiritually we may need to seek release from this hold which other people's past actions has over us.

Being close to a ceremony or activity where spirits are being invoked may be dangerous (1 Corinthians 10:19-20). It is vital for Christian workers to pray for one another often, particularly in times of stress, fear and political unrest. Openness with one another, forgiveness and love will strengthen and protect us against Satan's attacks.

2. Follow Jesus' example
Matthew 4 describes how Jesus handled Satan's temptations. He recognised where the thoughts and suggestions were coming from, and so did not even consider them, although they perfectly fitted his situation (physical desire, recognition, ambition). He knew the scriptures, chose statements from them and applied them right into the temptation, so silencing each one. Then he commanded, 'Away from me, Satan!' And Satan left! Jesus submitted himself to his Father's will whom he had just obeyed (in baptism), and he was filled with the Holy Spirit. Remember that Jesus is now praying for you, and each of these steps is possible for you in facing your temptations.

3. Put on your armour
First of all, remember the truth that you are 'in Christ Jesus', chosen, accepted, loved, and even in a sense seated with him in the heavenly realms (Ephesians 1:1-2:10). Scripture gives us many promises of protection. Read often Psalms 18, 46, 121. 'The Lord is my rock, my fortress and my deliverer.' 'God is our refuge and strength.' 'He who watches over you will not slumber; The Lord watches over you.' Notice too Proverbs 18:10: 'The name of the Lord is a strong tower; the righteous run to it and are safe.' God has given us ample protective 'armour' (Ephesians 6:13-17). Paul's list includes a helmet to keep our minds at peace; a breastplate to protect from accusations; a belt of truth to hold us when lies and deception try to disrupt us; shoes to keep us steady and ready for action even in rough situations; a shield to keep Satan's fiery darts from getting into us; and a sword, the word of God to use accurately, with the Holy Spirit's power behind it. This armour is God's gift to us. Live in it at all times.

4. Pick up your weapons
We have three types of weapon. One is the Bible, God's Word, and a second is prayer. Both of these 'have divine power to demolish strongholds' (2 Corinthians 10:4). They are to be used *for* people, in building faith and encouragement, and *against* the enemy of

souls wherever he is at work. The Holy Spirit is our teacher and he empowers us as we speak and pray. It will be right sometimes to fast and pray to bring us more into line with God's purposes and authority.

The third type of weapon is the gifts God has given to the church for our equipment and spiritual warfare. We can ask God for them. Particularly relevant to spiritual battles are 'distinguishing between spirits', and 'speaking in different kinds of tongues' so that the Holy Spirit can pray through us in effective power (1 Corinthians 12:10).

5. Take Jesus' authority
Christ's authority never our own, is effective. He said, 'All authority in heaven and on earth has been given to me. Therefore go...' (Matthew 28:18). It is at the name of Jesus that every knee shall bow (Philippians 2:9-11; Mark 16:17). Jesus gives us the right to use his authority as we submit to him. It is given, not just assumed (Luke 9:1; 10:19). Jesus told his disciples that they would receive his empowering (Luke 24:49; Acts 1:8). They obeyed and acted on it right through the book of Acts. It is important that we know we have authority to meet situations of spiritual warfare, and we prepare for this by spending time with the Lord. For example, a police cadet has to submit to discipline and study, and gradually moves up the ranks gaining more authority. He can act with authority, arrest wrong-doers and know that the law will ratify his actions. So we are given authority to 'bind on earth' (i.e. to rebuke and stop evil) and to 'loose on earth' (i.e. to set people free from wrong bondages). This authority is ratified in heaven because it originates with Christ and is part of his work on earth (Matthew 16:17-19; Luke 4:18).

6. Get into the battle
As you get into your work, always praise God. Declare his power and greatness, sing to each other and to the Lord using 'psalms, hymns and spiritual songs'. Our faith is strengthened as we worship and praise (Ephesians 5:19; Colossians 3:15-17).

Build each other up in faith and expectation; let God's love and grace flow to one another (Jude 20, 21). Forgive and pray for one another, asking for the full equipment of God including the gifts of the Spirit, and the anointing of the Spirit for authority.

Declare over all you do and are that Jesus is Lord. Recognise and deal with sin and

hindrances in your own life. Keep alert to the Holy Spirit's promptings and obey them. Keep being filled with the Spirit. Claim the promises, protection, forgiveness, cleansing and authority of Christ. Claim his power as you pray that he will break the power of the enemy, and claim protection for your health and safety.

Pray for the place where you live, for its leaders and authorities. Pray against evil practices around you, violence, pornography, drugs, abuse, and occult practices including films and literature. Ask the Lord Jesus Christ to break their power, and always pray as a group for this. Pray too for the cleansing of your house and other buildings you use, especially when you first move in. Claim the power of Christ to destroy any evil power which may have been there. Destroy any signs of occult practice and dedicate buildings to the service of God and declare over them all that 'Jesus is Lord'.

Pray for deliverance for one another and especially when anyone is spiritually oppressed. The deliverance ministry is outside the scope of this chapter, but read the incidents in the ministry of Jesus and the disciples.

Always look for what God is doing and give him thanks. A grateful, appreciative heart will keep you positive and praising. Remember that the 'one who is in you is greater than the one who is in the world' (1 John 4:4). Finally, 'be strong in the Lord'. Satan is strong but the Lord is stronger. Keep your thoughts focused on the Lord and not on Satan or his work. Satan is not the cause of everything that happens; he is not that powerful. God is the one who is ultimately in control and he is steadily at work all the time. 'Magnify' the Lord to one another so that all can see how great he is.

Take courage; you are 'in Christ', in a living relationship with him, united to him. You are raised up with Christ and seated with him in the heavenly realms, that is in the place of victory and supremacy, far above all rule and authority. You have been made complete in Christ who is the head over every power and authority. You know his incomparably great power for us who believe. Christ is Lord over the principalities and powers; he created them, conquered them, is exalted over them and has rescued us from them (Ephesians 1, 2; Colossians 1, 2). So recognise your position in Christ, rely on him and ask for fresh supplies of his power through the Holy Spirit, to wage a good warfare, and having done everything to still be able to stand your ground.

CULTURE SHOCK

CONTENTS

PURPOSE

This Unit will help prepare you for the unnerving feelings surrounding Culture Shock, and will suggest some ways of dealing with it.

CROSS-CULTURAL STRESS

Cross-cultural stress is a common factor in living in a culture different from one's own. We have already seen some of the reasons for this. This stress is complex and affects different people in different ways – some apparently very little.

Cross-cultural stress has become popularly known as culture shock. This term was first introduced by Kalervo Oberg in 1960 and rapidly caught on. It captures the feeling of confusion and disorientation that many feel in a new environment. The article on pages 105-107 gives a clear explanation of the concept and the associated idea of a U-curve of adjustment.

There is no doubt about the reality of this experience, which so many have gone through. It can last six months or even longer. It produces emotional stress anywhere from mild irritation to deep bitterness. It is often evident when using public transport, or feeling overwhelmed by the lack of privacy, and in many other ways. It is helpful to know that others have had the same experience!

The limitation of the expression "culture shock" is that it can lead to an overemphasis on the psychological state of the person entering the new culture.

It can suggest that we somehow have a "problem" and need to "adjust". We have already discussed this in Unit 6. We saw there that learning skills is as important as changing attitudes. The reason we feel disoriented is because we are having to learn all over again how to fit in. So all the suggestions for learning social skills, language and so on will help us to do this. Slowly but steadily we will acquire the necessary skills.

We may know this in theory, but the problem is – what do we do when we feel disoriented or confused? That is what we are looking at in this Unit. And as we do so, we can remember that we were called by God to our new situation and that what we are experiencing is part of the cost of being His servant, enjoying always the additional assurance that He will help us through it.

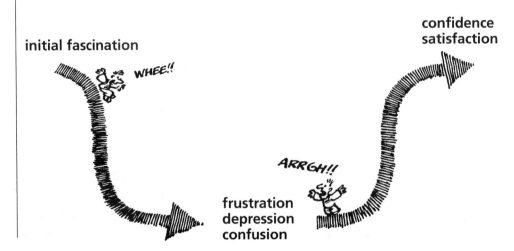

initial fascination   WHEE.!!

confidence satisfaction

ARRGH!!

frustration depression confusion

WHAT IS CULTURE SHOCK?

David Burnett

In your first week at a new school or college, or a new job, people were busily moving from one place to another, doing different things, while you were uncertain as to what you should be doing or how to do it. The people knew each other, and spoke to each other using terms and abbreviations which were foreign to you. Gradually you began to find out who people were and what was expected of you, and eventually you came to feel at home in the new situation.

Do you remember the emotional strain of those first few days until you became accustomed to that new environment? The sort of stress you felt at that time always accompanies a move from a familiar environment to another which is completely new. When you move from one culture into another completely different one you will experience the same form of stress, but it will be ten times, or even 100 times, greater.

This emotional stress in moving to a new cultural environment is popularly called 'culture shock'. The expression originates from the experience of many soldiers on the battlefield — 'shell shock'. Most people experience stress in adapting to another culture, but do not let that fact deter you from seeking to adapt to it. The experience of living and working with another group of people will be an exciting adventure that will bring you, and them, much blessing.

The causes of cultural stress
We usually regard our way of life as being the normal, reasonable way of behaving. Any deviation from this pattern is regarded as abnormal and therefore unknown and even threatening. We can determine our own cultural 'norms' by asking such questions as:

■ How do I dress for a particular situation?
■ How do I behave in that situation?
■ What do I believe?

When we are living in a situation within our 'norm' we will feel 'at peace' with it. The 'norm' may be likened to a road along which a person feels comfortable as he walks. On either side of the road is a hard shoulder onto which he may occasionally stray, but beyond that is

Zone of experimentation

Zone of experimentation

the rough ground of totally new experiences. When we enter a new culture we quickly find ourselves outside our 'norm'. This is the basic cause of stress. We are required to assess our style of clothing or our form of behaviour in relation to the local situation. A person may be pushed into what he or she may regard as 'excess of norm' or 'deprivation of norm'.

The 'excess of norm' experience initially leads to an element of excitement, but also to fear of making a fool of oneself. For example, if we are from a 'supermarket culture', we will not automatically raise our hand to push open the shop door. We are used to some electronic device opening the door automatically. However, people not used to this will instinctively raise their hand only to find they are pushing the air, and feel very self-conscious in front of others.

Similarly, a man who has always worn a white shirt for church on Sunday feels very self-conscious when he first wears a coloured shirt for church. All people are willing to experiment to some degree, provided that it is not excessive. If the experiment is successful it may be adopted as part of the person's norm.

However, if the experiment is not successful, or if the person goes beyond this zone of experimentation, two things may occur: *shame*, which is embarrassment before others, or *guilt*, which is inward remorse. The mild embarrassment derived from wearing a coloured shirt when one has been accustomed to wearing a white shirt is only minor, but for the person concerned it is very important and causes considerable stress.

Take this example of a missionary newly arrived in Japan. 'I remember after having been in Japan only a couple of weeks, deciding to get used to driving in Tokyo as soon as possible. I went out by myself in an old van. I drove for about ten minutes and found myself entering a busy shopping area. There were no pavements and the road was narrow, and all my attention was taken up with not hitting anyone. Suddenly a policeman jumped off his little stool at the crossroads and began frantically blowing his whistle and waving his arms. Thinking that someone had robbed a bank or something I edged carefully along until the policeman ran in front of the van and brought me to a halt.

'I opened the window and his face glared at me and from his mouth flowed forth an excited stream of unintelligible sounds. A little crowd gathered and the policeman to his acute embarrassment realised that he was shouting at a foreigner. I could only sit in the car dumb as the little crowd gathered. The policeman began to shout, "STOPU STOPU, BACKU BACKU" and pointed in the direction I had come. Feeling stupid I backed down the road, probably to the talk of the town. I had been driving merrily up a one-way street the wrong way; I had not recognised the sign. I drove straight home and dropped down emotionally spent in the safety of my little room.'

We can easily sympathise with his feelings. Many other illustrations could be given to show the problems one may face in seeking to cope with even the most simple of tasks in a foreign culture.

Emotional stress also occurs when we are

unable to live up to our normal expectations. This 'deprivation of norm' occurs when we are deprived of those things which we regard as standard for our way of life. It leads to anything from mild irritation to a deep-rooted bitterness.

For example, a group of wealthy American tourists on holiday in Scotland were annoyed when the hotel into which they were booked could only provide them with a shared bathroom. They were all used to having private rooms with their own bathrooms. Missionaries may be faced with similar problems when they have to make do with outside pit latrines having known only flush toilets before.

It is often the small things that seem to cause the greatest aggravation over a long period of time. Western people often miss the niceties of a clean, tiled bathroom with running hot and cold water. A concrete slab on which to stand and a bucket of cold water can be equally effective to keep oneself clean, but it is not that to which one is accustomed. Westerners also find lack of privacy difficult in the Third World, and this may especially be true for young couples. These things will produce some irritation, but if the person has responded to a call to Christian service then he needs to be willing to make the necessary sacrifices. Jesus spoke of the cost of being his disciple on several occasions (e.g. Luke 14:25-35).

Seeking to live and cope within another culture always results in being pushed out of our norm. This continual process results in an increase of stress. A survey of missionaries in 1984 revealed that 50% found adapting to another culture stressful, and 25% spoke of it as being very stressful.

The stages of cultural stress

'Culture shock', the emotional disturbance which results from adjustments to a new culture, results in two main sets of problems.

First, you do not know the answers to even the most basic questions. Where can I post a letter? Can I drink the water? Do men shake hands with ladies? What does that gesture mean? What is that woman saying to me? These are questions that even a child of that society can answer and yet you are at a complete loss. No adult likes to be reduced to the level of a child, and yet this is what happens when you move into a new society, and especially one in which you do not know the language.

You can face this problem even in a country which seems to be outwardly Western. In fact the outward Western nature of the society may increase the stress because the differences take you unawares. As one American missionary working in Japan said, 'The most difficult problem for Westerners in Japan is just living here. You have to start from scratch like a child and learn all over again.'

Secondly, you lose 'cultural cues'. The term comes from acting. In any play the actors need to learn not only their lines, but the cues which indicate when they are to say the lines. They need to learn their entrances, and the motions which they are to perform. A failure to follow the cues leads to confusion not only for the actor himself, but for all those involved in the production. Likewise in an alien culture you can fail to understand the meaning of various actions or sayings of the host people.

A person comes to greet you, and you put out your hand to shake his, but you find he gives a deep bow. You realise that you have misinterpreted the cue. It is often small issues that cause the problems because these tend to build up and increase 'culture stress'.

Oberg (*Practical Anthropology* 1960, pp 177-182) wrote of four stages in a person's adaptation to this stress. His model came from a study of many people who went to work in foreign countries, and it has proved useful in understanding the emotions which they experience.

Stage one he called 'fascination' due to the initial sense of novelty in a new situation. The strange foods, noises, smells, and sights all excite the new worker in any country. At this stage the person is primarily an observer and looks at things with an almost academic detachment. This is the tourist stage where the person has little real contact with the people apart from through a guide who acts as a cultural buffer.

The second stage commences as the novelty wears off, and conflicts start as the person seeks to cope with the new environment. Being unable to predict what is going to happen causes increases in stress, often to the point of hostility to the new culture and its people. So Oberg called this stage 'hostility'. This may bring the person to a point of crisis.

'Humour' was Oberg's term for the third stage.

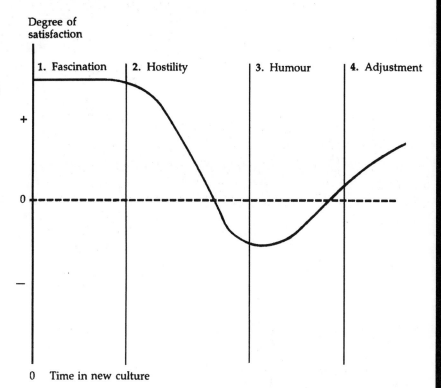

Eventually the person begins to achieve some of his or her goals, and this results in a growing sense of satisfaction and well-being. The person becomes more fluent in the language and instead of criticising the situation, laughs at his or her own mistakes together with the local people.

Stage four is called 'adjustment'. Here the person begins to cope reasonably well within the new culture although occasional moments of stress are still experienced. In general, however, the person is quite relaxed in the culture and able to deal with most issues.

We are all faced with stressful situations at one time or another. However, if the degree of stress becomes too high, as it may during stage two, we may seek to deal with it by various defensive mechanisms. This is natural, but in a situation of cultural stress it can cause additional problems.

The first sign most people show when faced with an excess of stress is irritation. It frequently occurs with language learning, which is why some writers have called this 'language shock'.

'Because language is the most important communication mechanism in a human society, it is the area where the largest number of interpersonal relationships lie. As the newcomer comes into a whole new world

where he knows no language at all, he is stripped of his primary means of interacting with other people, he is subject to constant mistakes, and he is placed on the level of a child again.' (W. Smalley, *Readings in Missionary Anthropology*, William Carey Library, USA 1974).

We may discharge the resulting tension by becoming aggressive towards other people or even things. Everyone knows of the husband who has a bad day at the office, and who takes it out on his wife at home.

Another way some people deal with tension is to withdraw from the stressful situation. They attempt to insulate themselves from the experiences with which they cannot cope. This gives rise to the 'mission compound' complex, when the missionary stays at home as much as possible.

It is very natural for us all to get homesick at times. Cultural stress can compound this natural feeling and produce an unhealthy attitude. It may cause an unhealthy pride in one's own country and the local people may interpret this as a criticism of their country. The local people will appreciate you more if they discover that you love both your own country and theirs.

SYMPTOMS OF STRESS

When we enter another culture our reinforcement mechanisms are taken away. The stable home culture which helps us to deal with stress is not there. Our initial response to living in a different culture may be excitement at travel, seeing new sights, observing strange customs. But this soon wears off and it is necessary to confront the daily reality of living as a stranger in a strange land.

There are various reasons why different people are affected in different ways.

1 The quality and length of preparation for the change. Also how much control you have over circumstances once you are there.

2 Personal characteristics, such as age, extent of previous travel, language skills, resourcefulness, expectations, personality type, tolerance levels, extrovert or introvert.

3 Biological factors, such as one's overall physical condition, special medical or dietary needs; how one's body copes with stressful disruptions in routines; the way in which one reacts to fatigue and to meeting members of other groups.

4 The extent of the difference between the home and the host culture.

5 Obvious factors like length of stay, climate and accommodation.

Other factors that vary have more to do with the job we may be doing:

6 Expectations from project colleagues, for example that the new "expert" will solve all problems overnight. We may have to deal with their disappointment when they find this is not so.

7 Our job experience may be different from what local people expect of us. Job descriptions are difficult to write and tend to emphasise the positive.

You might like to imagine you are in a foreign country experiencing culture shock. Try to write a letter to a close friend (think of a particular one), telling him or her what you are experiencing and how you are feeling.

Here are some of the ways in which we may feel stress. You may not feel all of these – or any of them! But they are all symptoms which different people have felt as indications of their stress. →

We feel we want to withdraw from the local culture because trying to adapt is so stressful. Local people may interpret this as pride or a feeling that we are critical of their country and culture. That can make us feel worse.

A tendency to want to "do" to justify being there, because we feel guilty about our weaknesses and ineptness, especially in a hot climate.

We feel inadequate as we compare ourselves with others. They seem able to do more.

Because we experience a conflict of values or identities, we feel incompetent in conversations.

We may experience a sense of bereavement, loneliness and loss because we have been deprived of familiar relationships, objects and surroundings, and the emotional support which our status or our job gave us. We may feel we have been shaken to the roots.

We feel overwhelmed by lack of privacy.

We may feel as though we are in a goldfish bowl where local people stare at us or appear to be watching our performance.

The need for conscious adaptation causes fatigue.

The feeling of being a baby in the new culture may pass into "a teenager" stage when we try to give the impression that we know it all, yet we are all inexperience and insecurity underneath.

We find it difficult to cope with our domestic life – limited fuel or water supplies, lack of gadgets, coping with local help for cooking and cleaning.

We feel confused, even distressed, because of the difference in senses of humour.

We feel confused about our role, role expectations and self-identity.

We feel under pressure to be constant and positive in our witness to local people, especially if friends at home write asking such things as "Has anyone been converted yet?"

16 WAYS TO COPE

WITH YOUR FEELINGS

When potentially stressful situations come up secure help and answers from insiders. Those who keep apart get an outsider's answer to an insider's situation.

Admit your needs and confusions to local friends and make it plain that you want to learn. People help people in need.

Don't grumble, but do share real pain with others.

Be aware that there may be cultural adjustments to make with expatriates of other nationalities. For instance Americans are generally much more relaxed and extrovert than the British. Both groups will agree that the British are introverted but they evaluate it differently. Britons see it as a respect for privacy. Americans label it as negative and sometimes as snobbishness, coldness and unfriendliness.

Positive attitudes and the willingness to observe and listen lead eventually to rapport and empathy with the culture. Negative ones lead to withdrawal and alienation. Which path will you choose to follow?

Avoid the temptation to run away psychologically and physically and create a mini-culture with family or other expatriates. If you do this you cut yourself off from the people of the new culture. It is better to plunge right in and experience life from the insider's perspective.

Relax. Take breaks if you can't cope with more tension. Don't feel guilty about it.

Have a hobby and make time to relax with it. Make sure it is different from your usual work. Keep up your world interest by reading. Get a friend at home to send you a good magazine regularly. Look out also for interesting publications and cultural activities in your new environment.

Set realistic goals and reduce activities if necessary. Don't compare yourself with others. Your personality and gifts are unique.

Adjust to the authority of the Christian leaders in the new culture. If their style of leadership is different from what you have been used to, it is not necessarily inferior. Don't necessarily agree to take up the first responsibility you are asked to do. They may feel they have to ask you because they assign status to you. You may be able to suggest a suitable alternative person instead, until you are all sure that a particular responsibility is the right one for you. (On the other hand, in some situations you may have to wait a long time before you are asked to do anything – it may be a year or more, until people feel they know you. Be patient!)

Develop a positive attitude. Praise God. Laugh with people. Laugh at yourself!

Don't be so anxious to identify with the local culture that you endanger your health. Follow sensible guidelines for maintaining your health – physical, mental, social and spiritual. The details will vary according to your situation. To be careless about avoidable risks to your health is irresponsible.

Don't make changes in the way things are done at work until you have made every effort to understand the local cultural system. Don't be surprised if people expect a more authoritative form of supervision than you were used to in your own culture.

Avoid worrying about the impression you are making. Instead seek to understand others and their situation.

One of the best ways to cope with emotional stress and other problems is to have a support group you can call on both in your home culture and your host culture. Arrange a support group at home with whom you correspond. Make friends in the new culture. Join a local church where you can call on people for any urgent assistance or just for a friendly chat. Christian friends in the new culture can become our closest friends. But don't associate only with Christians or you will find you have been cut off from the wider society which you have entered and want to get to know. Look for friends from other backgrounds as well.

Don't make changes in the way things are done at work until you have made every effort to understand the local cultural system. Don't be surprised if people expect a more authoritative form of supervision than you were used to in your own culture.

Forgive yourself when you make mistakes. Don't mope over failures.

INTERVIEWS

Ask your friend to recall for you the week in which he or she left their home culture and arrived in your country. Invite him or her to share his reflections on the experience of "leaving" and "arriving".
This could fit well into any of your sessions together.

BUILDING GOOD RELATIONSHIPS

Marjory Foyle

Christian workers overseas often complain that the amount of energy they expend trying to get on with each other reduces the energy available for the job they came to do. Behind the complaint is the naive expectation that Christians should live together in constant harmony. Yet the disciples quarrelled even when Jesus was physically with them. For example, James and John aroused the anger of the others through their status-seeking behaviour, and they all started arguing about who would be greatest in the coming kingdom. So it is hardly surprising that Christians today quarrel from time to time! What matters, however, is not so much that they quarrel, but what they do to resolve the quarrel and what they learn through the experience.

There are many reasons for poor relationships between people working together. Behind many of the upsets is the fact that everyone is different. This may threaten some people, because we like to slot people neatly into categories. When they do not fit the expected slot, our anxiety is aroused, we become defensive and the group becomes divided.

Then there is the problem of stereotypes, our preconceived ideas about people which are usually based on childhood learning. For example, most of us expect Texans to be boastful, Scots to be mean, the English to be snobbish and the French to be elegant! Before we even meet people, the mental stereotype is raised in our minds and we build defences against them. When we actually meet the people concerned they may not resemble the stereotype at all, which makes us more confused and defensive; they cannot be slotted in.

In overseas work, there are five basic causes of interpersonal relationship problems. Most of them are based on individual or group differences.

Physical causes

Dr C. B. Dobson points out in his book *Stress, The Hidden Adversary* that physical differences are responsible for some of our behavioural variations. Some people function best in the mornings, others in the evenings. Nervous people tend to be more anxious on the day after the weekly holiday, and better towards the end of the week. Confident people are the opposite. This is why staff meetings at the start or end of the week can sometimes be difficult — it is wiser to hold them midweek when both groups are at their medium best!

These differences can create tensions in a marriage. If the wife is a morning person, she comes down to breakfast neat and clean, dressed, and possibly made up. Her husband may be an evening person, so he slouches down grumpily to breakfast, and cannot bear her cheerfulness any more than she can stand his slovenliness. Unless they understand the origins of their differences, they may end up quarrelling bitterly.

We all work at different speeds, too; some people are quick and others slow. Difficulties can arise if the quick ones drive slow people to the point of exhaustion, or the slow ones hold back their quicker colleagues to the point of screaming frustration. Of course, physical differences should never become an excuse for unacceptably careless or slovenly behaviour, but understanding them can help us to organise our work and to be tolerant with each

other. Those who function best in the evening should plan easy routine work for the mornings, if possible. A similar arrangement can be made for spreading one's workload through the week. Both slow and quick people need to discuss their pattern with each other so that they are free to say, 'Don't hold me back', or 'Don't drive me'. In no circumstances, however, should we use physical differences as excuses for poor work or the inability to handle emergencies. This is one of the reasons why God gives his children extra strength!

Causes arising from our work

Friction between old and new workers is highly damaging to interpersonal relationships. Several factors are involved.

1. Fatigue and resultant over-rigidity
Older missionaries have often survived long periods of over-work, and they have coped by setting up rigid routines that more or less run themselves. Unfortunately, routines can get out of date, and the older person may be too tired or too out of touch to realise this. New people see what is wrong quickly, and with the best motives in the world may rush in with suggestions for change. Unfortunately the older person often interprets these as criticisms, rather than valid points. The result is that new ideas are brushed aside with the 'it's not the culture' excuse, which makes new people angry and frustrated.

New workers should note that they often (and quite unintentionally) make older staff feel inferior. It is all too easy for the older staff to get out of date, and the tragedy is that they may cover up with the autocratic 'Big Sahib complex'. Sometimes they may even refuse to teach their juniors anything as a result of their deep-seated fear of losing their position. If as a new worker you genuinely appreciate what has been accomplished, it will be possible to present suggestions without hurting anyone, and the genuine desire of the older people to learn new things will at once become apparent.

2. Jobs may not be what we expect
Job descriptions are notoriously difficult to write and often emerge heavily weighted towards the positive side without presenting the problems and weaknesses of the local situation. This is no-one's fault, it is just how the mind works. There is no point therefore feeling angry and frustrated at the realities of the situation: the perception by senior staff of well-established work can be just as rigid as the methods they use to accomplish it.

3. Conflict between spiritual and secular work
This can become a major cause of stress. Christian workers desire to serve people in the name of Jesus, and also to share in the ministry of the local church as opportunity arises. But they may feel so overloaded with professional work that there is little time or energy for anything else. This leads to resentment against the senior organisers who appear to condone the overload.

The only way to handle this is to avoid the secular/spiritual dichotomy which implies that some work is more spiritual than others. It is wrong to imply that the Holy Spirit is more involved in direct church work than in professional work. However, it is important to try to reduce the professional overload so that the worker can feel fulfilled in all areas of his or her ministry. One solution is to train many people to do small parts of the work, so that senior professionals are released from details to develop other aspects of their lives and ministries.

It is of course essential for you to maintain your personal devotional life, but this may mean changing long established habits. After several disturbed nights on the job, you will find it almost impossible to concentrate on praying and reading the scriptures. There is no need to worry about this — God is compassionate and loving, and well understands the needs of tired people. Jesus himself was tired after travelling. He can communicate with us through one short verse of the Bible, and we can talk to him through short telegram prayers, until we are less fatigued.

Administrative hassles
In the course of counselling Christian workers overseas I have found a strong link between their anxieties and the administrative structure of the sending organisation. If the organisation has a modern constitution which is reviewed regularly, personnel anxieties can be reduced. Policies which cover the smaller details of expatriate life help to avoid the frustrations which arise if small requests have to be sent back for individual decision by the relevant committee, which wastes everyone's time. It is much easier to have written rules, plus some escape clauses for emergencies!

It is also important to keep channels of communication and decision-making clear. Workers who know they will be consulted about things that are relevant to them, and who are regularly informed about what is going on, feel much more secure.

At the same time, workers overseas should remember that administrators can also have problems. Too often administrators become the targets of other anxieties which in reality are nothing to do with them. They too need to be respected and cherished. They need someone to talk to and periodic administrators' conferences are well worthwhile.

Cultural Clashes
Our relationships with one another can become strained simply because we come from different cultural backgrounds. Cultural beliefs and habits are usually learnt in childhood, so when we come up against totally different patterns of behaviour, a deep-rooted part of our make-up is attacked. For example, some Scandinavians feel it is wrong to send children to school before the age of seven or eight, whereas other nationalities send them to nursery school when they are three. This difference can become a bone of contention, each person protecting their own way of doing things as a part of protecting their national integrity. Similar differences arise over dress, manners, working patterns and domestic life.

Cultural differences between expatriates and nationals of the host country can obviously strain relationships. Expatriates who stay too long in the same place may hinder the development of local leadership, which is obviously resented. They can offend local customs through sheer ignorance, and while nationals usually understand and forgive, those who do not work so closely with the expatriates may cut off relationships with them. In some countries family demands impinge on working patterns. Expatriates, with their poorly developed tribal sense, may find this incomprehensible and irritating.

The only way to cope with all this is to

learn local customs as fast as possible, and then to remain in the humble position of 'having to learn' for the whole of your overseas career. Good humour over mistakes, a readiness to apologise, and increasing freedom in communicating with and relating to each other can result in wonderful friendships with local national colleagues.

Expatriates from different home countries may also experience relationship problems. Language can create major misunderstandings. Even if English is the mother tongue, not everyone speaks the same kind of English. For example, the British and Americans may totally miss each others' meaning despite communicating in English. Where English is the normal language of communication but is a second language for some of the expatriate team, the problem can be even worse.

Social customs differ, too. For some, Christmas Day may be the important festival; for others it is Christmas Eve. Great offence can be caused when we fail to understand each others' different patterns of professional training and the significance of the letters after people's names. Financial disparity may create conflict or embarrassment, especially when team members' children have grossly disparate possessions and lifestyles.

One of the greatest dangers facing expatriates, which can lead to mental ill health and group disruption, is the formation of a subculture. In isolated areas where expatriates live and work together as a separate community, some stress within the group may result in it becoming detached from the outside world. People over-concentrate on the internal problem and levels of stress and tension rise further. In an attempt to cope with this kind of conflict, a subculture develops in which certain patterns of reacting, behaving, and expressing Christian belief become the norm. Conformity to this norm makes individuals acceptable, whereas non-conformity leads to accusations of being unspiritual. The end result may be an epidemic of anxiety, panic, fear of other people's opinions, depression and an increasing inability to cope. As in a physical epidemic, the symptoms are infectious and the mental health of several members of the subculture may be adversely affected.

Two things will help you to avoid this danger. The first is to maintain a healthy balance between the expatriate group (if it has to exist at all) and the outside world by daily social contact and personal integration. The second is to care for every aspect of your personality. Taking holidays away from the job, keeping up an interest in the world as a whole, reading and continuing your hobbies, as well as keeping your professional knowledge and spiritual life fresh, will all help to diminish the subcultural danger. Be careful not to become preoccupied for too long. All Christians are periodically burdened for some special need, but this is not a permanent state of mind; the preoccupation usually gives way to wider interests. If it does not, then you would be wise to see a doctor, or at least to take a short holiday away from the work situation.

Personality Clashes

We can often have trouble getting on with people because we have different personalities and are at different stages of maturity. There are many complicated classifications of personality type and I do not intend to use any of them! Usually, we have trouble with other people's personalities because they are either too similar to or too different from ours. For example, two obsessional people who love order and neatness to the extent of becoming over-anxious if things are in a mess, may not be able to get along together at all. In fact they make each other worse. Two people with histrionic natures can rarely work together either. A dramatic outburst from one will often precipitate a similar response from the other! But mix the obsessional and the histrionic together, and the combination may be quite good.

The major difficulty overseas is that people may have to see too much of each other; there is just nowhere to get away from each other for a while. In such circumstances, it helps to remember that the other is the other, and that you are you. Both of you have a right to your own personality, but also a duty to try to curb its abrasive action on others. If it becomes impossible to live and work together, then it is better to split up and work with someone else.

This is just what Paul and Barnabas did after John Mark had caved in under the strain of the work. Barnabas decided it was his duty as John Mark's uncle to stay with his nephew, but Paul refused to take the young man. When they split, the Lord sent Silas to form a new partnership with Paul. It is encouraging to note that after a cooling off and maturing period, Paul and John Mark made it up and became colleagues again.

When we start thinking about our own personality type, it is so easy to feel that God has favourites. He seems to have given other people calm, placid and easy-going natures, whereas we may have to struggle with anxious or thorny personality structures. In fact, the other person may be having just the same struggle but they do not speak about it and it may not be so obvious. It is important to remember that God knew exactly what he was doing when he made us, as Psalm 139 says. Our personalities can get marred during their development but as God works with us to overcome the problems, we end up stronger people because we have had to struggle.

An important aspect of anyone's personality is its maturity. Immaturity can have profound influence on personal relationships. Erik Erikson taught that personality develops in eight stages, something special being learnt at each stage. Things like basic trust, personal identity, and the importance of being industrious are all related to different stages of personality development.

Some people, due to serious problems at a particular stage of their development, may not complete the necessary learning. For example, they may never have learnt all that is necessary to establish basic trustfulness of others. This usually does them no harm, for they learn enough to manage. However, if several areas of their personality are underdeveloped, immaturity can result which causes trouble not only to the individual personally but also to their capacity to build relationships. This is frequently accompanied by persistent negative emotions such as bitterness, resentment, jealousy and hatred. These cause much unhappiness to the person concerned and to colleagues.

I have found it beneficial to teach people the importance of handling persistent negative emotions. Take jealousy as an example. People can be helped to identify the times in their lives when they experienced severe jealousy. Often, these are related to childhood experiences. To begin to understand why other people provoked such jealousy, to develop compassion for those who hurt them and to be able to forgive them, can be a healing experience, which in turn leads people towards maturity in the damaged areas of their lives.

Unit 12

TAKING THE PLUNGE

PURPOSE

This Unit will help you with your initial experience of beginning to live in another culture.

LIVING AWAY FROM HOME

OBSERVATION

In this Unit you are invited to "take the plunge" and spend some time living with people of another culture. It is written on the assumption that you will be staying for five days or so with people of another culture within Britain.

It may be that you are in fact going abroad, perhaps for a couple of months or even longer. It may be that you are going not just to learn from the experience but to serve Christ in some particular way. If so, the material in this Unit will help you in your early days and weeks there.

> **The main purpose is to experience living in another culture, and to observe and learn as much as you can.**

■ On the basis of your experiences you will also reflect on your response to people of other cultures and other religions, and the role of the church in that situation, as it is and as it should be.

■ You will also consider possible ways to communicate the gospel with people of other cultures and faiths. You should mix both with Christians and non-Christians from that culture if possible.

There are no required activities for this period of cross-cultural experience. You just need to take every opportunity to find out about and to experience the new culture. A great deal will depend on your hosts and you will need to fit in with what is convenient for them. Be careful to explain to them why you are doing this and what you hope to gain from it – almost certainly you will find them extremely helpful.

HEALTH

If you are going to travel to part of the 'developing world', you will need to take care of your health in various kinds of ways. For a helpful guide, get *The Travellers' Good Health Guide* by Ted Lankester who is Director of Interhealth, a health charity specialising in the care of aid workers and volunteers.

As you take part in your daily routine and activities, your first task is to observe as much as possible. The things to observe are the things that we have noted already. This will include:

👁 **Social Structures**
See Unit 6. The questions on page 58 may be appropriate, but are very much geared to rural situations. So don't use them if not appropriate.

👁 **Social Skills**
See Unit 6 again. You will have a good opportunity to observe and to learn some of the social skills of the new culture. Don't hesitate to ask your hosts about the things you see and questions that arise. People do not usually mind newcomers asking questions. And if your stay is comparatively short, then it will not matter too much if you make some mistakes!

👁 **Roles**
The roles of men, women and children are always interesting to observe in any culture.

👁 **Language**
See Unit 9. This might be a good chance for you to try out some of the principles suggested there. See whether you can pick up some words and phrases from a different language. Try out the GLUE method and see whether it works.

👁 **Culture**
Consider the way the culture looks at things – things like time/event, status, tasks/relationships, judgment. See Unit 10. Look for examples of these different orientations.

Talking to people is a very good activity and you should take every opportunity you can to do this. Of course, you should not presume on people's time unnecessarily, but you will probably find that people are willing to spend time to talk. You can ask again some of the questions that you have asked in your interviews with your friend. Pick out appropriate questions and note down the answers, either at the time or later.

You may have opportunity to ask people about their religious faith, following the questionnaire

guidelines. This could also be a very good opportunity to visit a place of worship. In some cultures, such as the South Asian communities, it may be possible to visit more than one place of worship.

THE CHURCH

During your period of cross-cultural experience you should specifically think of the mission of the church in that culture. If there is a church or a Christian fellowship in that culture, then you should arrange to visit it, attending worship if this is possible and practical, talking with Christians from that culture or working in that culture, and generally observing and reflecting on what kind of impact the church is making.

KEEPING A JOURNAL

It is important to spend time each day reflecting on your experience and writing things down. *Inside Story* is an example of someone who did this. How do you feel about the things he says? What surprises you? What do you particularly identify with? Or feel awkward about?

INSIDE STORY

Ian Wallace

21 JAN **I've Arrived**

I'm not really sure what I expected this place to be like. It's certainly different from anything I have ever experienced. It is different, too, from the pictures I have seen of the Third World — somehow they seem to depersonalise everybody and give the impression that people are just waiting to die. Here there is life and the people are real. I was not struck instantly by scenes of appalling poverty as I thought I might be although I was amazed that even a city this size mostly has mud huts. There is so much that is new and interesting. Even the hour-long wait at the airport while someone found a customs official didn't seem too bad although I suspect such things may prove to be a source of frustration once the initial interest has worn off.

24 JAN Slow Food

I am beginning to get used to the heat now — I couldn't understand at first why I had so little energy but obviously the heat had much to do with it. It is not a heavy heat but is just as if someone was pointing a hairdryer at me all day long and gradually all the energy I had at breakfast evaporated.

Raising the subject of breakfast I might as well mention my confusion over the different times of the meals out here. On my first morning I got up expecting breakfast to 'happen' before work started — it doesn't and the other expatriates are obviously so used to breakfast after doing three hours' work that it didn't occur to them to tell me.

I went to the market for the first time this morning — it was full of noise and colour and movement. I wonder if I will find England a bit drab after my time out here? I tried my luck at bartering — I'm not sure if I made a good buy but everyone had a good laugh at my faltering attempts to name a lower price. Mercifully the money is fairly easy to understand although I haven't a clue how it compares with the English pound.

12 FEB An Adventurous Motive

When I spoke about my motives for going abroad at Christ Church before I left last month, I must have sounded super-spiritual. I am sure that love and a desire to see justice done are among my motives but I realise that many of the expatriates are here because they enjoy travelling, and I am no different. It's nothing to be ashamed of; rather it seems that God has used my sense of adventure to lead me here and to equip me for whatever difficulties I have to face. I am sure that not everybody is suited for this sort of life no matter how concerned they are for the needs

of the poor. However, my interest in this new culture has helped me to cope with the strangeness of the past three weeks.

I am looking forward to moving into my house — it isn't finished yet. I don't mind staying with others — it has been a good way of getting to know them but I would like to unpack properly. I still await the arrival of my other luggage from England. Stupidly I used some of my socks to pad out the gaps and now I am short of socks! I don't think I will really feel at home until I have a place of my own.

19 FEB Homesick

I felt my first twinge of homesickness today. I was listening to one of my favourite pieces of music when my mind drifted back to an afternoon in mid-January spent walking the dog on the Downs. It seems such a long time ago.

I wasn't able to brood for long, for at that moment one of the Christian Youth arrived. He had simply come to visit. We spent a pleasant fifteen minutes together but I was clearly more embarrassed by the silences than he was. For the first time I have felt the frustration of not really knowing the language. In church someone always translates but here I was on my own and I realised how limited I was. I must get on and learn the language — how else am I really going to share with the people I have come to serve?

3 MAR The Weight of Poverty

Today, I had an insight into the burden of poverty which people have to live with. On the surface you do not see their poverty for the Africans are jovial and get on with the job of living — that is why up to now I have been blind to the circumstances which they have to cope with in their daily lives. It was Luarte who first opened my eyes to what their poverty is really about. His wife is pregnant and collapsed while carrying water from the river. Neither of them had eaten for two days, preferring to give what food they had to their two-year-old. It seems that the price of sorghum had gone up in the market leaving many people hungry. Luarte's wife has been diagnosed as having severe anaemia but there aren't the medical

facilities to help her. The child is due next month — I pray it will be delivered safely. I feel that my work has acquired a new significance — I so want to help people like Luarte and his wife, but am I doing any good?

22 MAR A Place of my own

At last I have moved into my house and immediately set about trying my hand at baking bread. Life here seems to be a cross between camping and what it must have been like living in England eighty years ago. I had not encountered weevils before and now I understand why it is so important to sieve the flour. Unfortunately I must have killed the yeast as the result of my efforts was a brick rather than a loaf. I have been approached by a Sudanese lad who has offered to do the housework — I don't know whether to take him on or not. I reckoned I could cope on my own and the thought of having a servant seems rather paternalistic. Yet I can't deny that I feel extremely tired and I haven't started the washing yet. He did seem so enthusiastic about the job and I suspect he won't find work if I don't take him on. I shall have to think more about it.

13 APR Doubts

What am I doing here? I feel like a fish out of water. We come from abroad with big heads thinking we have all the answers but I can't see that I am doing any good at all. I can't even speak the language — it just doesn't seem to come, apart from a few glib greetings. And I don't know what possessed me to lose my temper with Jacob. I despair of myself sometimes.

14 APR Loneliness

Yesterday was a bad day. I think tiredness was part of the problem but I do feel low at the moment. I yearn for a good friend to talk to — to share my doubts and concerns. I am sure that God wants me here but I'm having to learn slowly and painfully that working with other Christians is not always a joy. There is much that I still have to learn about working overseas. I don't have all the answers to all the problems — that much is abundantly clear. I can also see that it is easy to do more harm than good by being too hasty. There are no simple solutions to the problem of poverty and it takes time to understand what really lies at the root of the problem. Yet I am sure that there is value in encouraging our Christian

brothers in the face of their difficulties and providing the resources to help them escape from the chains of poverty.

Jacob came to me at breakfast and we talked for a long time about our families. I believe he could be a good friend.

29 MAY — People before Projects

Today we heard a report that the army has mutinied and already people are talking of civil war. It made me think how insubstantial much of our work is. One mortar could destroy a newly built clinic. Yet in recent weeks I have seen changes in the lives of one or two of my friends. That is something which men cannot destroy. Perhaps this is what Paul meant when he compared our work either to hay or wood which burns up or to stone which withstands fire. No doubt when I get home people will want to know about the wells that have been dug and the buildings that have been erected but I recognise now that these are not the most important aspects of our work.

7 JULY — Beggar my Neighbour

I am ashamed of myself. I call myself a Christian yet could not even spare a crust for the beggar who called this afternoon. I had plenty of excuses at the time — it was the last bit of bread I had and there wasn't time to bake more. The excuses seem very flimsy now. The money I gave him for a cup of tea was an insult to him and was simply the easy option for me — where is Christian love in that? There are so many beggars and I am frightened of being known as a 'soft touch'. There are also people who are equally poor who don't beg. Lord, what am I to do?

15 JULY — An Extravagant Gift

I have just got back from a weekend 'in the village'. I was invited to join a pastor on a visit

to a refugee church and it has left a deep impression on me. Just before we left one of the refugees disappeared momentarily and on his return present me with a chicken. This is an extravagant gift from one so poor yet it was given so joyfully and unashamedly. My mind immediately went back to the old beggar who I turned from my door. I feel that today I have learned something about the true meaning of generosity. Next time the beggar calls I will try to greet him more graciously.

2 OCT — Delegating Responsibility

I had the opportunity to see my co-worker cope with a problem on his own today. He wasn't aware of my presence and just dealt with the situation. I must confess that I was surprised how well he coped. Whenever I am around he carefully allows me to take charge and so has not had the chance to show his potential. The time is coming soon when he will need room to 'stretch his wings' and gather experience in shouldering responsibility without me around. I must be ready to move on from here soon and leave him to it. I'm going to find it hard leaving these people whom I've grown to love so much, but it is for their own good and that is the paramount factor if I am truly to be a servant to them.

10 JAN — Hard to Leave

The lump in my throat is hard, my heart is full with emotion and I am struggling to hold back my tears. I can still see my friend through the aircraft window and I feel as if I have left something of myself there. The last few days have been full of farewell parties. They were almost too much for me. Everyone enjoyed themselves to the full yet each was sad because we were shortly to be separated by a great distance. I wonder whether I will ever see these friends again? My thoughts remain with the Christian Youth who gave me a card which was filled with farewell messages. Yet I am sure that it is right for me to leave — the job God gave me to do is done. He calls me on and I must follow. My co-worker, the Youth, my friends, must all be given room to grow to maturity. I suppose I feel much as a parent must feel when a child breaks free of the home. My co-worker needs his independence; he has learned to manage on his own.

4 FEB — Back in the Cold

England seems so cold. The temperatures are actually quite mild — it's the people I'm talking about. Everyone is so busy going about their business that no one smiles or says hello — I feel alone, frozen out by the fact that everyone ignores each other. I held out my hand to shake someone else's, forgetting that the English don't shake hands in the same way that they did overseas. The chap wasn't expecting it and it caused embarrassment on both sides. At least we were able to laugh about it.

Everybody seems so pale and ill. I hadn't realised how used I'd become to the rich dark African skin. Our society lacks the colour of Africa in every respect — drab overcoats take the place of bright kangas. I suspect I'm being unduly harsh on the English — I need time to adjust to England again and time to work out my sense of loss. I suppose this is what they call 'reverse culture shock'.

15 FEB — I'm different now

I went shopping today and had to give up. I found I just couldn't make a choice. In Africa soap was soap but here it's either Palmolive or Boots or Imperial Leather or Shield. What's the difference? — how do I choose between them?

Various things have surprised me. People seem to drive so fast and yet I always reckoned that I was a fast driver. I am continually amazed at how little people really understand the problems of the Third World. I have to do a talk at Christ Church on Sunday and I don't know how I'm going to explain what I've learned in a faithful yet simple way. I'm not sure it's even possible because I no longer share the same concerns as most of those around me — there seems to be a gulf that separates us. I do wonder if I shall ever really be the same again.

KEEPING A JOURNAL

It is important to spend time each day to reflect on your experience of that day. You should make notes on the different areas mentioned above, in a notebook or file which you keep specifically for this period of cultural exposure. In it you will write down your observations: the things you see, but also your reflections on the things you have observed and experienced. You should allow 1-2 hours a day for this. It will be an important part of your learning. You will also use this journal to reflect further on your experiences later.

Inside Story is much briefer than the kind of journal entry you will write for each day of your short stay in another culture, but it may give you a feel for writing down your thoughts and experiences.

Here are some questions to ask yourself at the end of each day, as you write your own journal. It will be helpful to use these questions every day, though you will not answer all of them each day.

? What did I do today? Make a brief record to remind yourself. Include things like the conversations, the questions you asked, the answers you were given. It is important to recall the events, replaying them in your mind and in your journal.

? Who were the interesting people I met today?

? What did I most enjoy today?

? Did I have any funny experiences today?

? What was the most difficult/ frustrating experience today?

? What did I observe today about the new culture?

? What have I found that was different?

? What have I found that was similar to my own culture?

? What was surprising?

? What assumptions did I find myself making today regarding
■ the people of the new culture?
■ people of my own culture?

■ the culture as a whole?

? Did I find some of my assumptions mistaken?

? Has anything made me rethink my attitudes to people, culture or myself?

? What are some things I would like to learn more about tomorrow or in the future?

? What are some of the things I want to pray about specially, with regard to today's experience?

The articles on the following pages may help you with the personal and spiritual difficulties that living within another culture can bring.

DEALING WITH DEPRESSION

Marjory Foyle

Whether or not you habitually suffer from 'depression', it would not be surprising if you experienced it occasionally overseas. Many people have bouts of 'feeling depressed', a kind of sadness which is a response to situations that we find unpleasant. A few suffer from a 'depressive illness' which has definite symptoms, and may require medical treatment. These different aspects of depression need different approaches.

Feeling depressed

Certain things are likely to make expatriate workers feel depressed. The commonest is loss. You gain much when you go overseas, but equally you lose much. In leaving home, you lose the sense of security that comes from living in a familiar culture. During language study or when starting a new job you may lose self esteem. Later on, the loss of trusted colleagues who return home on leave or who retire, the loss of a loved location when you are transferred somewhere else, and the repeated loss as children go off to boarding school, are common features of expatriate life. Not everyone, of course, feels depressed at such times, but many quite naturally do.

In order to remain healthy and useful, you need to learn how to handle these reactions. One way is through mourning or grieving. So important is this that Freud called it 'the grief work', indicating that there was something definite to do before adjustment was achieved. Unfortunately, Christian workers often think they are being weak or unspiritual if they feel depressed after a loss. I have known expatriate mothers who kept apologising for weeping when their children went back to boarding school, as if they were doing something wrong.

The scriptures give us a role model for 'grief work' in the account of Jesus in the garden of Gethsemane. While none of us grieves so severely or for such a purpose, the incident teaches us that mourning can be creative and can accomplish that which is needed to enable us to go on in God's service. Jesus had accepted a human body at the time of the incarnation, and he knew that his body was to be the means of accomplishing the salvation of mankind. In the garden he was partly mourning for the loss he would experience in the next few hours. He was working through his grief, to come to terms with it and to make a new act of acceptance. I believe he was also mourning the loss of his relationship with the Father that he would experience on the cross, the loss of his human friends and the pain of betrayal, and the loss of human dignity as his body was exposed publicly and humiliatingly.

The Lord experienced great emotional pain; the Amplified New Testament translates Matthew 26:37 as, 'He began to show grief and distress of mind, and was deeply depressed.' This was not a depressive illness, but a strong human emotion, permitted for the purpose of accomplishing the grief work. He was then strengthened for the task ahead of him, for at the end of his grief work he was able to arise and say to his disciples, 'Rise, let us go! Here comes my betrayer!' (Matthew 26:46). Of course we cannot take the analogy of Jesus' experience too far, but it does indicate that mourning is a creative act. So there is no need to feel ashamed if you grieve after a loss of some kind. Rather, welcome it as a way of coming to terms with the situation.

It may help you to understand some of the normal stages of grieving so that your feeling of depression is not totally bewildering. After a loss of some kind, the first thing that happens is that your mind denies it, as a kind of immediate emotional first aid. For example, if we hear that a trusted and valued colleague is leaving, the first reaction is 'Oh no, it can't be true.' The second reaction is anger. We feel let down, angry because our colleague has been taken away and we shall have to cope with everything. This leads to the third stage, a sort of bargaining. We begin to pray, 'Lord, if only you will let him stay here I will be able to pray more, or teach a Sunday school, etc.' But finally the situation is accepted; we begin to think how the work can be reorganised, and make definite plans for coping. This indicates that the mourning process is nearing completion, and we can move on to the next stage of our life.

While you mourn some loss, do not be ashamed of feeling depressed and upset. It is never right to let our grief disrupt other people's lives, but it does help to talk about it with a friend, to mourn and be comforted, so that we can go on with our ministry. An expatriate friend of mine had to go to the station to see people off as part of her job. She said she never got over the feeling of depression that hit her every time as the train moved out, but she recognised it as one way of coming to terms with her repeated bereavements.

You may also feel depressed after certain illnesses. Dengue fever, hepatitis, and various types of flu can all leave an aftermath of depression which persists for several days. Another potent cause of depression is fatigue, due perhaps to over-work or to lack of care for the whole person. Keeping hobbies and holidays, regular time off, wide interests and hard work on the job in a well balanced pattern of life are vital if you are not to feel depressed too often. And under-girding all that is a healthy spiritual relationship with the Lord, through prayer, Bible study and church attendance. But do not be worried if your spirituality seems at a low ebb from time to time. The Lord fully understands that we are overburdened and can minister to us through a few short verses and a brief prayer.

When the work load becomes too great for us, the mind often uses a trick called denial to help us to cope. The mind simply blots out the realities of the load and its wider implications, so that we can focus on the present moment. Many workers in extensive famine areas use this trick subconsciously. They think only of the baby they are trying to save at the moment, not of the millions behind the one baby. Such a device is one of God's gifts to enable hard-pressed workers to cope, but it should not be abused. Some people stay for too long in such high stress areas, and eventually the defence may break down and symptoms of anxiety or depressive illness emerge. Hence it is essential in any overloaded, high stress situation, that limits to exposure are set and that withdrawal for rest is made a part of the relief programme.

Situations that make us feel helpless because we have no control over them can cause people to feel depressed. This is particularly so if little beneficial result from the work can be expected. It is even worse if the work may actually cause harm and we have no control of the outcome. For example, some poorly organised aid programmes are like this. The workers realise that large amounts of aid can lead to dependent peoples, and they have to struggle to communicate this to the donor agency. This explains why it is so important to have worker representation on central donor committees; such policies help reduce depression by increasing workers' participation in project control.

What to do when you feel depressed

1. Accept that it is normal to feel depressed when something important to you has been taken away. This is normal mourning and should subside. If the emotional pain is still reducing your ability to cope after six weeks, then seek medical advice.

2. Take great care of the whole person. Learn to play, to keep your mind active, to care for your body, and to care for your spirit despite limited time.

3. Do not worry about working in extremely difficult situations. 'Mental denial' will operate when the pressure is great, narrowing your interest to the task at hand. But do have a fixed programme for rest, even if it means leaving people in need and pulling out for a time.

4. Discuss any feeling of helplessness with the local leader and your friends. If your personality reacts badly to having little control of the situation, consider asking for a change. Someone with a different personality structure may cope without difficulty. This is nothing to be ashamed of — one man's meat is another man's poison!

Depressive illness

An illness called depression may attack a person, making him or her unable to cope to their full capacity, or sometimes unable to cope at all.

Workers with depression need to see a doctor, but often their colleagues do not know the kind of symptoms that make medical care essential. Important symptoms are an inability to cope with work, increased or decreased sleep, loss of appetite, poor concentration, being slowed down or unusually restless and anxious, crying too much or being unable to cry at all even when it would be expected. In addition the sufferer may have multiple guilt feelings often over trivial things, feelings of being worthless despite evidence to the contrary, and a loss of religious faith.

Everyone has some of these symptoms from time to time, but if they persist for more than three weeks, or if they are very severe, then help is needed. When several of these symptoms are combined, a doctor should be consulted. People who make suicidal threats should never be ignored or handled purely spiritually; they must have a medical consultation as well. In any isolated area it is better to consult a doctor too soon than to stay on for too long in the remote place.

Treatment of depressive illnesses of this kind starts with a careful physical examination, for it is important to exclude possible physical or medicine-related causes. Then, suitable anti-depressant medication will be prescribed. People get worried about taking such tablets, calling them drugs and fearing dependency upon them. But antidepressants do not cause dependency, and do actually cure the illness.

As the depression improves, discussion about personal stress becomes important. It must be remembered that not all depressions have entirely psychological causes; some have a strong chemical element, hence the relief obtained through medicines. But the efforts made to cope with the illness often prove stressful in themselves and this, together with discussion of any other forms of stress, needs a thorough airing. One area of special importance to consider is that of interpersonal relationships with colleagues, spouse, and children. Sometimes relationships in the home country need attention. Anything that causes true guilt needs to be dealt with, but remember that during the height of the depression there may be a lot of untrue (morbid) guilt that need not be discussed. It will settle as the illness comes under control.

Another kind of depression afflicts those who have felt inferior and inadequate for most of their lives, and who have been hindered from reaching their full potential because of such feelings. The *Shorter Oxford Dictionary* defines depression as being 'put down' and this is a feeling common to sufferers from this type of depression. In a few cases, expatriate life is helpful to such people, making them feel wanted and useful. Often, however, they have so much trouble in adjusting and making new relationships that depression may be precipitated. Such people usually have difficulty getting off to sleep, and a tendency to feel anxious and depressed in the evenings, which is unlike other kinds of depression.

Sufferers from this form of depression can be helped by a few simple things. There is usually a lot of anger involved in the illness which has been turned inwards rather than being released outwards in a healthy way. The following advice may prove helpful.

■ *Relieve the immediate depression by diversion.* This sounds stupid, and involves making a little effort, but is often worthwhile. Taking a walk, doing something creative like carpentry or painting (the house or on canvas!), going to the movies, playing a game, may all help to externalise anger through activity. Sitting brooding on your own failings and inadequacies is the last thing that you should do.

■ *Reaffirm your trust in God* who loves to help those who have no further personal resources to tap. Remember that he is

standing with you in the effort to develop your personality and will truly help and advise throughout.

■ *Discuss with a close friend areas of your life that need to be strengthened.* Do not go round a series of people asking this question, but ask one or two. Take these things to God, asking for his help.

■ *Look out for any permanent negative emotions.* These are things like persistent anger against someone important to you, jealousy, persistent resentment and bitterness, and hatred. It is of course important for everyone to get rid of these, but they do play a significant part in people who persistently feel inferior. Do not brood about these things: instead ask God to remind you of any important ones, and wait for him to show you. People with this kind of depression should not sit brooding or poking around their minds to try to find their negative emotions! If they are important, then God will remind you of them.

Much has been written about the importance of forgiving those who hurt you, and this is especially true when you are handling negative emotions. For example, resenting for many years someone's actions against you can damage your mental health and well-being.

Everyone therefore should be careful to get rid of persistent negative emotions, and forgiving the other person is usually the best way. People suffering from depression often find such an act very beneficial. It is not usually necessary to take it up with the person concerned, and anyway they may have died before the matter is dealt with. It is wisest to make an act of forgiveness as a matter between you and God alone, leaving him to work as he wishes in any other people concerned.

THE POWER OF HELPLESSNESS

Cathy Humphries

There is an abundance of new encounters in those first few weeks. I felt that no amount of reading, talking to people, seeing slides or photos could have prepared me for the 'baptism' that was to ensue as I stepped from the heavenly detachment of the plane flight: overwhelming mugginess that clothes you with its steamy heat; smells of burning charcoal, car exhausts, open sewage, body heat; explosions of colour in clothes, flowers, painted vehicles; the throb of people everywhere; the noise of the city, crickets and frogs at night, voodoo drums, death wails. Like a mind subjected to the plunges of heavy rock, the body cannot tolerate detachment and the beat becomes your own.

Reflection on all that you have seen, heard, smelt and felt comes a little later. It is often painful and costly to stop and think, but it also bears its own kind of fruit. I remember taking a walk into one of the shanty areas of Port-au-Prince near where I was staying, shortly after my arrival in Haiti. I had never met face to face with such living conditions — such a mess of cobbled together 'houses', open gutters, and somehow men, women and children living there. I felt guilty, angry and frustrated. I had winged my way from reading, preparation, an orientation course, a myriad vaccinations, and an exciting and expectant farewell service at my home church which emphasised 'sending out for service in the Third World'. Now I was looking into the face of the 'Third World' in utter helplessness.

However, looking back I feel that helplessness and vulnerability are key ingredients, sent out as we are in the power and name of the Lord Jesus. As Thomas Merton has written, when 'we stand alone before God in our nothingness without explanation, without theories, [then we are] completely dependent upon his providential care, in dire need of the gift of his grace, his mercy and the light of faith' (*Contemplative Prayer*). I wanted to move away from that place of helplessness so quickly. It is difficult in the early days: we have no defence in words or in activity. Communication in the local language is faltering or non-existent and even deciding how (and what) to buy in the market and how to cook it will possibly have to be surrendered to someone else. Everyone seems to be rushing around yet you cannot do anything yet.

At times such as these, pointlessness and loneliness can make rapid advances. Yet at these crisis times God can work with such great power. On reflection I felt my own thinking was (and to some extent still is) heavily weighted towards activity, progress — turning away from the feelings of failure, weakness, vulnerability. Yet the key Christian truth of the cross is rooted in what I class as negative. There at the heart of God we see a 'limitless, precarious and vulnerable love' (W H. Vanstone). There we see the vulnerability of Jesus, his absolute dependence and obedience to his Father and a love of powerlessness. It is the quality of this love that does not threaten or force, but where it is encountered it draws out a free response.

So soon, it seems, into our assignment, we start to become 'able' and inevitably get drawn into the mêlée of activity. Most of it is good activity, but it can take us away from dependence on God and on those around us with whom we have come to share Jesus' love. It was through the Haitian people that I realised how much more activity-orientated I was than people-orientated. It seemed to matter more to them who I was than what I did. As I thought about this, it seemed to me that serving and helping in the developing world came down to one-to-one relationships. That does not mean writing off projects but putting the emphasis on people.

Again Thomas Merton has put it very well: 'Do not depend on the hope of results... you may have to face the fact that your work will be apparently worthless and even achieve no result at all. As you get used to this idea, you start more and more to concentrate, not on the results, but on the value, the rightness, of the work itself... gradually you struggle, less and less for an idea and more and more for specific people. In the end, it is the reality of personal relationships that saves everything. The real hope is not in something we think we can do, but in God who is making something good out of it in some way we cannot see.'

This learning to see what God is doing is fundamental to our Christian lives anywhere. The point we often forget amidst all the need is that God is at work. Our joy is in being asked to join in. The price is high, but it buys something magnificent.

RELATING TO THE NATIONAL CHURCH

Bill Roberts

Jesus told his disciples to be servants of one another, to 'wash one another's feet' (John 13). Everyone should wash the feet of others, and at the same time should expect to have his or her own feet washed by others. There must be give and take in every fellowship if it is to grow in a healthy manner, just as there must be in a marriage relationship or any other close friendship.

As you join in with the local church of the country to which you are called to serve, you will have something to contribute. You will also have much to receive. Both giving and taking must be built on genuine humility if a deep and Christ-like relationship is to develop. Many missionaries have gone out full of the zeal of giving but not balanced by that humble need to learn from, and be built up by, the national church. The first fundamental element of any good relationship with the national church is to be ready to listen to, and to

learn from, all that is good in it. Jesus also commanded his disciples to 'love one another as I have loved you' (John 15:12). If sacrificial love is coupled with genuine humility, then there is no limit to the way in which your relationship with the national church may develop.

Relating to individuals
Every fellowship is made up of individuals. The more you get to know and understand them, the better will be your working relationship with them. During my twenty years as a missionary in West Africa, I discovered two particular ways of developing this relationship.

First, it was developed by practising hospitality within our own home. We usually had two or three secondary school boys living with us at any one time. This not only gave us a wonderful opportunity of discipling them in the

natural surroundings of a Christian family, but it also taught us much about Africans and their culture. It also became obvious to everyone that we loved Africans. Because we ate African food, lived simply, and did most things the African way, Africans felt free to visit our home. This further built up our relationships with individuals. It also prevented us from falling into the old danger of making the missionary home into a little corner of England (or America) in a foreign land.

Secondly, we built healthy relationships by receiving hospitality from Africans. My work required me to travel a great deal, so as I planned these tours I looked for opportunities to stay in the homes of African Christians. When I, as a white missionary, received hospitality from black Africans – and obviously enjoyed it – our relationship was enriched beyond all measure. Once again, the give and take principle was at work.

You not only give to a relationship but also receive from it, and thus a balanced growth takes place. Of course, there will be some difficulties as you experience different food, cultural practices and standards of hygiene. But you soon learn that just because something is different, it is not automatically inferior. You may even come to realise that all those coats of paint you put on the walls back at home, along with the frequent changes of wallpaper and floor carpets, were nothing but a huge waste of God's money.

I have always been impressed by the way in which Jesus the Jewish man asked the Samaritan woman for help – 'Give me a drink'. A relationship between two people will never develop if one side is always giving and the other is always receiving. But if you receive with genuine humility and give with sacrificial love, then you are going to make many deep friendships amongst Christians whose background may be totally different from yours. Whether they come from a rural or urban setting, whether they are educated or illiterate, rich or poor, black or white, matters not. As long as they are 'in Christ' and you are determined to practise the give and take principle, then you will surely experience some very meaningful relationships.

Relating to the local fellowship

You may be the only Western person in a little village church, or you may worship in a large multi-racial city church. Whatever your situation, make sure you become a part of the local fellowship in the deepest possible way. The writer to the Hebrews says, 'Let us consider how to stir up one another to love and good works, not neglecting to meet together, as is the habit of some' (Hebrews 10:25). This fellowship is necessary in our home churches, so how much more necessary it is when we are living in another land.

In simple terms that means taking part in as many activities of the local church as possible. In practical terms that may not be easy. You are probably going to be very busy. You may live many miles from the nearest church. There may be a language problem, and you may not even find their church activities very meaningful.

But however busy you are, and however far away from the church your home may be, you must make time to be present at Sunday services and mid-week fellowships. This is as needful to you as it is encouraging to the local Christians. You may have to travel a few miles, but it will be thoroughly worthwhile; besides, it is not unusual for Africans to walk several miles to church. If the language used is not English, then you must take time off until you can converse in the common language.

Sometimes the way the church conducts its activities may seem strange. You may not be used to services lasting two or three hours, or sermons lasting well over one hour. When I arrived in Africa aged twenty-nine I had never attended a funeral service, and would not have expected to unless a very close relative or friend had died. Now I entered a society which placed enormous emphasis on the burial of the dead.

All-night vigils, in which large numbers of people would visit the home to sympathise with the bereaved, were time-consuming and costly occasions as everyone expected to be fed. Each day before and after the funeral would see the deceased's home full of visitors. Sometimes they would be chatting, sometimes saying nothing. The body had to be put on display, after a costly process of preparation. Relatives would fly home from overseas commitments at great expense just to be present at the funeral.

Very expensive coffins were thought to be essential to show due respect to the deceased, often leaving the family with a large debt to pay off. The funeral service itself would be full of platitudes, sometimes not true and often grossly exaggerated. The post-funeral activities sometimes included attempts to make contact with the departed spirits, although the local Christians would not take part in this.

At first I saw little which was of value in these costly and time-consuming customs, but I gradually came to appreciate some of them at least. A visit to the home and attendance at the funeral were expressions of loving concern to the bereaved and of respect to the departed. The converse would be seen as an insult to both the bereaved and the deceased. Hence each of these customs was an accepted way of expressing love and concern within their society and within their church life, and if I was to be seen as a loving, sympathetic and concerned Christian, I would have to take part in them too.

If some of the bereaved family were committed Christians then there would be ample opportunities for a positive Christian witness to be made to the visitors who were coming to the home. There are many people in Africa who have found Christ through such events. So do not be too hasty in devaluing local church customs. With time you will see their strengths which will help you to build a more meaningful relationship with the local church.

Relating to church authorities

The principles for this are just the same as in the local church. Pray for leaders, get to know them, become a part of the life of the church, make yourself available for any kind of service and be willing to submit yourself to their authority. Perhaps it is the latter that a foreigner finds most difficult, until their latent superiority complex has been crucified. We have to appreciate that just because someone's style of leadership is different, that does not necessarily mean it is inferior.

There is often a great variety of church leaders with vastly differing abilities. Some are humble, mature men of God whose authority is easy to accept, others may be very difficult to work under. Some may be highly organised, and others have little organisational ability. This can be frustrating but the Westerner who is timetabled-orientated can learn a lot from those who are people-orientated. Some leaders are highly educated, others are not, and the Westerner must realise that wisdom does not only come from formal education. Some leaders are rich but many are poor; your tithe may exceed the total giving of the congregation, in which case you may be wise not to give it all to the one cause.

Whatever kind of leadership you may find in the local church, be as supportive as possible. Then you will develop some good relationships and may even be given some special responsibilities. But do not allow yourself to be swamped with responsibilities which someone else should be encouraged to take. If you have any problems with the church authorities it would be wise first to ask the advice of a mature local Christian with whom you have developed a trusting friendship, rather than to go straight to the person concerned. It is always desirable to have a close friend in the local church with whom you can share and pray over any problems that may arise; such a friendship may prove to be invaluable.

QUIET TIMES FOR RISK-TAKERS

Pauline Hoggarth

'Our Lord did not say "I am come that ye may have safety and have it more abundantly". Some of us would indeed give anything to feel safe, about our life in this world as in the next, but we cannot have it both ways: safety or life, we must choose.' (Gerald Vann, *To Heaven with Diana!* pp 51-52.)

As followers of Jesus we can live our lives well within the boundaries of what is safe and familiar and comfortable; or we can respond to the Bible's invitations to live riskily, pushing out the frontiers of our faith, exploring new territory in God's company. 'Choose for yourselves whom you will serve...'; 'Follow me....'; 'Take up your cross...'; 'Preach the good news to all creation'; 'Do not conform any longer to the pattern of this world...'; 'Love one another...':

these are all invitations to live the richly unsafe life God offers us. And it's not necessary to go overseas as a missionary in order to live riskily in this sense: in fact, if we haven't started to explore here and now the possibilities of life, in the sense Jesus meant it, we probably shouldn't be thinking of going overseas. We can't begin to love and serve our neighbour and be open to learning from him across the barriers of language and culture until we've learnt to cross some barriers here. We shouldn't need to leave our home patch in order to be involved in what Paul called the 'ministry of reconciliation' (2 Cor. 5:18).

Our willingness and capacity to live riskily depend on the quality of our relationship with God — on the nature of our spirituality. We

can't give out to others more than we are taking in from God: if we try to do so, our ministry will very quickly become hollow and unreal.

Three different kinds of spirituality

What kind of relationship with God, then, will set us free to be people who may be 'often troubled, but not crushed; sometimes in doubt, but never in despair... though badly hurt at times, not destroyed'? That's how Paul describes himself in 2 Corinthians, (GNB), a letter that's all about the experience of risky living for God. In his exploration of this letter, *A Spirituality of the Road*, David Bosch describes three different kinds of spirituality:

1. The 'Pilgrim's Progress' type is defined in terms of the time we spend *away from* the hurly burly of the world and its demands on us. It's a spirituality of withdrawal, if you like, a recharging of the spiritual batteries so that we can go out into the world to love and serve our neighbour. 'So many minutes of spiritual exercise will give me so much mileage for the day that follows' (Op. cit. p. 11). This may well be the pattern with which many of us have grown up — a spiritual slot at the beginning of the day (or perhaps at the end) which doesn't seem to have much to do with what happens in the rest of the twenty-four hours.

2. The 'Jonah' type of spirituality doesn't take us out of the world; it throws us right into the turmoil of it. We're so concerned to love our neighbour and reach out in service to others that our vertical relationship with God somehow gets squeezed out. We become anxious activists, and soon burn out because we're not drawing on God's resources.

3. The third pattern for our spirituality holds tightly together our dependence on God and our call to be involved in the world and love and serve others. Our model is to be found in the cross: 'The cross is, in one sense, a sign of total identification with the world. Jesus was never more worldly than on the cross. In another sense, it is a sign of radical separation from the world. Jesus never stood over against the world more clearly than here. *Spirituality is both of these at the same time.*' (Op. cit. pp 15-16.)

On a journey with God
This third way of relating to God and the world is a 'spirituality of the road'. If we're practising it, we'll have understood that the Christian life is a journey with God; we'll take seriously the words of Psalm 84:5, 'Blessed are those... who have set their hearts on pilgrimage'. We'll be willing to explore, to be open to new ways of knowing God, expecting that he will change us. We'll want to hold the happenings of our daily lives and the events of our world open to God's word, as we reflect on it; our conversations in prayer with God will be about today's stage of the journey.

This kind of relationship with God will protect us from the twin dangers of missionary life: the danger of becoming sloppy and lazy and ceasing to have any sense of direction and purpose, or the danger of becoming *driven* people, who are over-active and try to prove themselves by the amount of work they do. Instead we will be 'living in a gentle tension between giving ourselves in full surrender to our fellow man, yet at the same time enjoying the peace of the Lord. The Jesus who said "If anyone wishes to be a follower of mine, he must leave self behind; he must take up his cross and come with me" (Matthew 16:24) was the same One who said "Come to me, all whose work is hard, whose load is heavy; and I will give you relief" (Matthew 11:28). It is simultaneous "double movement" again: going into the world and coming out of the world.' (Op. cit. p. 23.)

So how do we go about it?
How can we make sure that our relationship with God and our relationship with the world (values, decision-making, work, friendships, sharing our faith, service, leisure, church activities, use of money, political attitudes and activity, reading, etc) are held closely together in that 'double movement'?

In the first place we need to look honestly at the state of our spirituality *now*. We may need to be open to changes; perhaps we're locked into some system we learned a long time ago, when we were new Christians or children. The idea of change in our relationship with God may feel very threatening; we may even feel guilty about it. This is all part of the pain and the joy of spiritual growth. We recognise that as we grow older, we change and develop and have different needs. But sometimes our spirituality remains static and rigid; it doesn't grow up with us. Different personalities come to God in different ways, and we need to be set free to explore our own way, learning from others, but not feeling guilty if we don't conform to their approach. 'All indicators point to a close relationship between our innate temperament and the type of prayer best suited to our need. Introverts will prefer a form of prayer different from Extraverts (the terms are those of the Myers-Briggs personality test)... Feelers pray in a different way from Sensers... As we grow in maturity and learn to make good use of all our abilities in functioning and relating, our prayer life should become richer. While we may still prefer the type of prayer that matches our natural temperament, we should familiarise ourselves

with the other forms of prayer that have been developed over the centuries.' (C P Michael and M C Norrisey, *Prayer and Temperament*, p.16).

Whatever our temperament, there are some specific and practical ways in which our time with God can be helped to 'grow up'.

1. Specific times and 'one the hoof' prayer
Perhaps you've had some bad experience of a very rigid or legalistic approach to spending time with God in prayer and reflection on his word. This may make you reluctant to think again about setting specific time aside each day. You find much more attractive the idea of praying as you go about the ordinary affairs of everyday life. But without a definite daily time set aside to focus our attention on God, our 'on the hoof' prayer will be shallow and perfunctory. There is evidence in the gospels that Jesus had a habit of daily (and usually early) time with his Father. 'If we have faith enough to realise our need for regular prayer, and courage to persevere, then we shall be open to receive a very precious gift of God: a condition of heart and spirit in which an awareness of God's presence is never far from our level of consciousness, so that we revert to his presence frequently, naturally and joyfully.' So says Sheila Cassidy in *Prayer for Pilgrims*, a book I specially recommend.

If the idea of committing yourself to a daily 'quiet time' frightens you, and you think you'll fail to keep it up, try setting yourself a reasonable period to give it a go (six weeks is a realistic time). Tell someone else about your commitment and ask them to pray regularly with you about it. Trust yourself to God's grace: it's sufficient for you, in this as in everything else.

2. The Bible keeps us real
You may even have had some negative experiences with the Bible. Perhaps you've seen it used to manipulate people; perhaps there are parts of it that are painful for you, or make you angry, and you've never had a chance to talk about them and express your doubts or fears. Don't let this experience have the last word. Don't avoid those hard bits — open them up to God. Tell him how you feel, what you don't understand, ask advice from Christians you trust, be prepared to do some work on the difficult bits of the Bible. All this is important, because when you go overseas, many new voices will shout at you, you'll be caught up in new situations, have to think about different values, experience new and perhaps difficult relationships. You may be

tugged at by persuasive people, and find it hard to decide priorities. You'll need to be able to measure and evaluate all these experiences against something objective. For the Christian, that objective yardstick is God's word. As the Holy Spirit applies it to our lives and opens God's thinking to us, we'll learn to understand the events of our lives in its light, and it will give depth and stability to our responses.

3. Recollection

This simply means reviewing, usually at the beginning of our time with God, the happenings of the last twenty-four hours, and looking ahead, as far as we can, at what the next twenty-four hours may hold. It will help if we make notes, and jot down our feelings about these events: Do we fear them? Look forward to them? Not know how to respond to them? Did we enjoy them? How did we see God's activity in them? Did we take bigger steps of faith this time? As we reflect on God's word (whatever system of Bible reading we use), we can hold these events up against it and expect God to help us to see them in a new light, give us unexpected insights, evaluate them in his way.

4. Intimacy

When Jesus said 'Remain in me, and I will remain in you' (John 15:4), he was talking about closeness, about intimacy between himself and us (Henri Nouwen, *In the House of the Lord*, p.8). As human beings, we long for intimacy, and yet we also fear it. We ache to know and be known at a deep level by another person. But the process of opening ourselves up, of becoming vulnerable, of disclosing ourselves to another, of being willing to listen to another, frightens us. Sometimes we're not willing to take the risk, so our relationships remain on a superficial, often deeply unsatisfying, level. Sometimes we take the risks and experience the overwhelming delight of growing in understanding of another, of being heard, accepted, loved.

In our prayer life with God this process of intimacy is often short-circuited. We've been taught that God is all-knowing and all-seeing. So we don't bother to put into words our fears, longings, feelings, joy, loneliness, thanks. Or, just as in a human relationship, we may be fearful of opening ourselves, or not prepared to make the effort. Think of the most important and intimate relationship you have; imagine if all communication in it were pared down to grunts and nods, shopping lists, yeses and

noes. Compare your prayer life to this. If your praying is as impoverished as this, you may need to do something about it.

'My heart says of you, "Seek his face!" Your face, Lord, I will seek.' (Psalm 27:8)

Intimate prayer can be 'on the hoof' prayer. As well as those times which we set aside specially to concentrate on God, we can recollect the events of our lives and talk intimately about them to the Lord when we're on the bus, cycling to work, doing the ironing, changing a wheel, bathing the baby. As we deliberately turn our minds and hearts to God, intimacy with him will become more and more a part of our lives, and we'll begin to realise that the old 'compartments' have gone, our lives are more of one piece, and that unconsciously we're holding together our relationship with God and our relationship with our world.

Some further practical suggestions

1. Parents of small children can often feel very unspiritual, because of the difficulties of finding time to be quiet with God. Learn to be flexible, don't feel guilty, ask God for times of intimacy with him at unexpected moments.

2. Going overseas is an opportunity to enrich your spirituality by reflecting on God's word in the company of people from another culture. Make sure you are reading the Bible in community with others as well as on your own.

3. Ask God to give you at least one friend from the culture you are working in, with whom you can pray and reflect on God's word. Be prepared to trust and learn from him or her – not just from your expatriate colleagues.

4. Before you go overseas, take some practical steps to make sure you have a variety of resources to draw on. Most of us need some kind of structure for our time with God: Bible reading notes, a calendar of daily readings, will help you. They need to be ordered, or you should ask a friend to send them regularly. Perhaps you might like to try a less familiar translation of the Bible.

5. Take with you a few books to enrich your spiritual reading. Broaden your horizons with some poetry (from George Herbert to Steve Turner); dip into *The Lord of the Journey* (Roger Pooley and Philip Seddon), or some of Henri Nouwen's books

(*Reaching Out, Creative Ministry*); try some of the spiritual classics: Brother Lawrence's *The Practice of the Presence of God*, St Augustine's *Confessions*, Julian of Norwich's *Revelations of Divine Love*: look at J. I Packer's *Knowing God* or Eugene Petersons's *Run with the Horses*, Richard Foster's *Celebration of Discipline*. Take a couple of biographies: *Surprised by Joy* by C.S. Lewis or Joni Eareckson's books.

6. Experiment with keeping a journal: this may be a combination of diary and notes from your quiet times — your recollection jottings, prayer reminders and answers. In times of loneliness or stress, it can be a tremendous help to write down your feelings. At other times, you'll be encouraged to look back on the evidence of God's activity in your life. And you'll enjoy the creativity of writing.

7. Most people find it helpful to go back to the same place to spend time with God: the familiarity helps us to settle down in God's presence. In some countries, you'll be able to go outside. You may find the bathroom will be your place, or the car, pulled off the road!

8. It's worth thinking about your physical posture when you're reading and praying. Practise consciously relaxing the muscles of your body and face. Find a posture which helps you to be alert and relaxed in God's presence. Feel free to reflect the moods of your prayer with physical gestures (for example, as you intercede for people, you could hold your hands up to God as you hold these people up to him; if you feel angry, clench your fists; express joy and worship of God in ways you feel comfortable with).

Above all, as you look honestly at your times with God, and at the quality of your spirituality, be encouraged. God loves and accepts you; Jesus died for you and pleads your cause with God; the Holy Spirit prays for you when words fail. The call of God to serve him overseas, whether short or long-term, offers you a new opportunity to reflect on your spirituality and accept the need for growth and change. Take it with both hands.

'Praise be to God, who has not rejected my prayer or withheld his love from me!' (Psalm 66:20)

FINAL REFLECTIONS

At the end of the five day period you should work through these questions again, this time answering each of them for the period as a whole.

PERSONAL REFLECTION

You should make some personal reflection on your experience of living in that culture, how you responded to the different experiences and how you feel about your own response. You can make use of the reflection questions in the guidelines for your interviews. In particular ask yourself:

- How do you feel about your own response to the people of that culture?
- What did you find the most enjoyable?
- What did you find the most difficult?
- Do you think that you would like to live in that culture if you had the choice?

- What are the areas in which you feel you have grown as the result of this experience?
- What are the areas in which you feel you need to grow more?
- What would you do differently if you were going through the same experience again?
- What lessons have you learned for the next time you go to a new culture?

THE MISSION OF THE CHURCH

You should also reflect on the mission of the church in that culture: as it is, as it should be. Here are some questions to which you should try to answer:

- What is the church like in that area and culture?
- If you attended the worship, what struck you about it? What was different from worship you are used to? Was this because of denominational differences or cultural differences?
- How do you feel about your experience of fellowship with Christians in the other culture?
- What is the style of leadership of the church in that culture? Again, does this reflect denominational differences or cultural differences?
- Do you find any connection between the style of leadership within the church and leadership in general in that culture?
- How do you evaluate the ministry of the church in that culture? Do you think that it is

effective in communicating the Gospel there?
- Do you think that the Gospel is being communicated effectively to that culture? Try to identify ways in which the Gospel has been adapted to that culture. If you do not think that has been done effectively, give examples.
- As you think of the ministry of the church and the communication of the Gospel in that culture, what suggestions would you give to the church there? If no church exists, how would you go about starting work in that culture? What form do you think the church should take? How would you present the Gospel? In what specific ways would you try to adapt the Gospel to that culture?

INTERVIEWS
AND
REPORTS

CONTENTS

INTRODUCTION

What kind of person should I meet?

The person you meet should be from a different culture, preferably with a different mother tongue from yours. Since your purpose is to learn about an unfamiliar culture, the greater the cultural difference between you, the better. So it may not be appropriate to choose somebody who has lived in your culture for a long time.

International students are a good choice, since their stay in your culture will have been relatively short. There are around 100,000 overseas students in Britain for higher education at any one time. They are often familiar with the idea of research and will usually not mind being asked questions. And they are very much in need of friendship. Even if you do not achieve all the goals of this module, to make friends with one international student is a worthwhile goal in itself! The majority of overseas students are men, and tend to be older than British students; but more and more women are coming to Britain to study – and remember that the men sometimes bring their wives, who often want friends and have a good amount of free time. There are also many recent immigrants in Britain whom you can meet and befriend. It is in general wise for you to interview somebody of the same sex as yourself.

How do I find somebody?

You may already be in touch with people of another culture. If not, here is some advice from the ISCS booklet *Adventures in International Friendship* (pages 3-4). It is written with evangelism amongst international students particularly in mind, but the suggestions are useful in your situation too:

Use your natural opportunities. People from other countries may live in your neighbourhood or block of flats. They may be enrolled in classes with you or work in your company. You may meet them at a shopping centre, launderette or while sightseeing. Find out what is being done for overseas students at your local college, polytechnic or university. If they have a "welcome" programme or a friendship family programme, volunteer and help.

Ethnic, religious and international student groups sometimes sponsor dinners and cultural programmes. They may be advertised in local circulars or newspapers and are often without charge. You will be welcome, and attending such programmes can give you an opportunity to meet people from a particular country or culture, and increase your knowledge of the world.

In a number of locations, the Universities and Colleges Christian Fellowship have active outreach programmes for overseas students through the Christian Unions. UCCF may be able to refer you to people in your community who are involved.

Two useful addresses if you need help in contacting international students:

- ISCS, 3 Crescent Stables, 139 Upper Richmond Road, London SW15 2TN (020 8780 3511) <info@iscs.org.uk>
- UCCF, 38 De Montfort Street, Leicester LE1 7GP (0116 255 1700) <email@uccf.org.uk>

Two useful publications may help you in making other kinds of contacts:

- *Faith to Faith Resources Directory* lists organisation and individuals involved in helping Christians relate to those of other faiths in the UK. Available from Carrs Lane Church Centre, Carrs Lane, Birmingham B4 7SX (0121 633 8860).
- *Directory of Asian Ministries* lists Asian Fellowships and concerned individuals, arranged by counties and London boroughs. Available from Asian Books, 50 Grove Road, Sutton SM1 1BT (020 8395 8281)

Purpose

The purpose is not at this stage to share your faith with that person, but to begin to understand and develop a warm and friendly relationship. Of course, if you develop that kind of relationship with someone, there will come a time to share with each other what is important for you both. It will be a natural outcome of the relationship. But our purpose is simply to develop relationships based on understanding, acceptance and respect for each other's different world.

You will need to explain this clearly when you first meet and make arrangements for your interviews. If you are contacting the other person for the first time, you can explain that you are making a study of culture and that one of the requirements is to interview a person from another culture. That should provide sufficient explanation and basis. Remember that friendship is the key to understanding and relating to people of another culture, so it will be good if your meetings provide the basis for real friendship, as well as giving you the information you want. But that cannot be programmed or forced.

When should I begin?

You can begin any time, but you will find it helpful to study Units 1-4 before you start your interviews. Particularly read the material on attitudes to people of other cultures.

Practical DOs and DON'Ts

Here are some practical ways to show love and courtesy and to build relationships of trust and acceptance.

1. Remember that the person you are communicating with is a person and should be treated as such.
    - Show courtesy and respect.
    - Try to understand the person as well as possible.
    - Remember that as well as being a product of a particular culture your friend is also an individual.

2. Show genuine interest in your friend.
    - Write down their name. Spell it correctly. Try to pronounce it properly. When you are on your own practise saying it.
    - If your friend is from overseas use your atlas. Learn a bit about their home country by reading or asking questions.
    - Try to get beyond the superficial. You may find it helpful to write down some information so you don't forget it and keep on asking the same questions.

3. Remember that your relationship is two-way and practise both sides of give/receive, talk/listen, teach/learn and entertain/visit.

4. Be culturally sensitive and remember that love does cover a multitude of mistakes. If you are really friendly and open people will forgive you for these.

5. Remember that cultures are constantly changing and that there are tensions everywhere between the traditional and the modern. If your friend comes from a modern or urban culture, it may be very similar to yours, at least on the surface (though there may still be significant differences at deeper levels). So don't ask questions that imply that their culture is "less advanced" or express surprise that it seems "very modern". Of course it is – it is just as modern as yours!

6. Write down the answers you get to the questions, and be prepared to discuss your reflections (on all three sessions) with your supervisor.

CULTURE INTERVIEWS

CULTURE INTERVIEWS

Take some time to introduce yourselves and explain the purpose of the interview, if that has not already been done. If the other person has come to your house, it will of course be appropriate to serve tea or coffee or other light refreshments. If you are meeting in a cafe or other public place, you should be the host.

Explain that you want to ask questions about a whole range of activities, (as required by your studies) as this will help to give you an insight into the other person's culture. Most people will not mind this, but it is worth saying that you do not want to ask anything too personal, and that there is no need to answer any question which seems to them to be embarrassing or which they prefer not to answer.

Explain that you will note down answers in your notebook, for the purpose of your study. However, be sensitive about this. If your friend appears ill at ease about it, or you find it difficult to concentrate, leave the writing and make notes afterwards. In any case, listening and observing is more important.

Introductions and general questions
Here are some suggested questions to begin with, not necessarily in this order. You can rephrase them, as appropriate, and add supplementary questions. The main purpose is to get to know each other.

1. Please tell me about your family? The members: parents, brothers and sisters, others. (You will ask in more detail later: this is just preliminary information.)

2. Tell me about your home: the house you live in now? the one in which you were brought up?

3. What is the climate like in the place where you grew up?

4. Do you come from an urban or rural background?

5. Have you always lived in the same place? Has your family moved about? Is your pattern the normal one in your culture? Are there many patterns?

6. What are you doing at present (work, study etc.)? What brought you from your cultural background into this one where you are now?

7. Tell me about the food in your culture or community.
   - what are the main foods (and what are your favourites)?
   - how is food cooked in your home?
   - when you eat at home does someone serve the food or do you pass the dishes around?

8. In your culture how do people greet each other when they meet, and how do they say "goodbye"?

As you get the answers to these questions (and others below) you can also share your own answers. But be careful not to talk too much! At this point you may like to ask about the experience of leaving one's own culture and arriving in a new one. Or you may prefer to wait and ask about that when you feel you know each other better. But sharing about this experience will be a good way of getting to know each other better.

Festivals

1. Do you celebrate birthdays in your family? If so, how?

2. What other festivals do you celebrate: in your family, in your community? Find out as much as you can about the festivals, the customs, food etc., and their meaning and significance. If they are religious festivals, find out the background.

3. What are the public holidays in your culture/country? Are they the same as the festivals?

Family (detailed)

1. Please tell me the main relationships in your family. How far do these relationship go: e.g. father, mother, grandparents, father's brothers and sisters, cousins.

   (Don't assume that these are the same as in your own culture, or use the same words as in English. For example "cousin" is used in different ways in different cultures. "Aunt" or "uncle" in English includes both your mother's and father's sisters or brothers. In other cultures these may have quite different names. In some cultures your father's older brother may have a different title from his younger brother, and so on. If possible, make a chart to illustrate the different relationships.)

2. What mutual responsibilities do the family members have? Who will take care of your parents when they are old? What happens if somebody is unemployed, or needs help to go to school or college? To whom would they turn?

3. In your culture do adult children live with their parents until they marry? If not where do they live? Do they and their spouse live with their parents after marriage?

4. Who looks after children? How are they disciplined? For example: "Scolding and spanking a child helps him to learn." Do you agree?

The next set of questions is about marriage. Depending on your time you can include them in this session or keep them for session 2. You will probably have covered enough material for this session. Remember to thank your friend and make arrangements for the next two sessions.

REFLECTION

After the session, record your reflections while they are still fresh:

1. What was new to you?

2. Did anything surprise you?

3. How much was familiar to you (seemed to be the same as in your culture)? Does this show that your cultures are similar in some respects? Or does it just reflect our common humanity?

4. Was there anything you found hard to understand or accept? Why? Do you think you would find it easy or difficult to live in your friend's culture?

5. Is the family structure very different? (Family is an important key to understanding another culture).

Marriage customs

This could be included in Session 1, if you have time. But don't hurry over it: this will help you to understand family relationships and structures.

1. In your culture in general, who decides about the choice of marriage partner (e.g. parents, all the other relatives, the young people concerned, a joint decision). Is it different for girls and boys?

2. Who are the eligible persons for marriage? Who are forbidden (e.g. first cousins). Are there any preferences?

3. In your culture how and where would a person meet their future spouse?

4. In your culture is it difficult to marry someone of another social or ethnic group?

5. Who makes the arrangements for the wedding ceremony?

6. Tell me what happens at a wedding ceremony in your culture.

7. What kind of agreement is made between the individuals/ families? Are there any gifts? Dowry? Exchange of property?

8. Where will the couple live after marriage?

9. What will be the relationship between the two families after the marriage?

10. Are marriage customs changing in your culture? Is this a good thing?

11. Do you think the modern dating system is a good system for marriage preparation Why, or why not?

12. How do young people prepare for marriage in your culture? Do you think this is adequate?

13. What about sex outside marriage? What are the common views?

14. What happens when there are marriage problems? Would the   family members intervene? What are the traditional solutions? Are these changing?

Community relationships

1. Which do you think is more important – the wellbeing of the group or the wellbeing of the individual?

2. In your culture you have an appointment in the Doctor's office at 2.00pm. What time would you plan to arrive? What time would you expect to be seen by the Doctor?

3. How do people spend their time? What are the main forms of entertainment?

4. What is the educational system in your culture? Is education considered to be important?

5. What about work? How do people choose their work? Do they have a choice? How is unemployment viewed?

6. What are the roles of younger and older people? What causes tensions?

7. What is the role of women in your culture and has it changed in recent years?

8. How do people communicate? (letters, telephone, newspapers, radio and TV, word of mouth)

Leadership and dispute settlement

1. Who are the leaders and famous people in your culture? (e.g. politicians, entertainers/sports personalities, religious leaders, older people, young people, media people, aristocracy/royal family)

2. How do they become leaders? (e.g. by election, achievement, wealth, birth)

3. What kind of authority do they have?

4. How do they use it and how do they keep it?

5. How are conflicts resolved? (e.g. political, religious, financial, property, legal, personal matters)

6. How do you decide at what level conflicts should be resolved
   - in the community as a whole?
   - among families?
   - between individuals?

7. What do you think is the most appropriate form of government in your culture? (e.g. monarchy, one party democracy, multi-party democracy, theocracy, rule by a strong leader)

REFLECTION

As before, write down your reflections on Session 2 as soon as possible.

1. Use the same questions as for Session 1.

2. Look back to your reflections on Session 1. Do you want to change any of your answers? Why?

3. Do you feel that you have begun to establish a relationship of trust and acceptance with your friend? Is there anything further that you can do to establish such a relationship?

Remember to give as well as receive, to share yourself as well as asking questions. Be aware of the issues in Units 4 and 5 on building relationships.

CULTURE INTERVIEWS

SESSION 3

Social Structures
Use the questions on the last page of Unit 6, if they are appropriate. (They are very much geared to a rural community. You may be able to transpose some of them to an urban setting, or you may feel they are inappropriate for your friend).

Social Skills
Pick out some of the areas from Unit 6 and ask how they would be handled in your friend's culture. You can share your own responses to some of them, if your friend is interested. This should be a useful exercise, because all cultures are constantly changing and your friend will be able to give you an accurate idea of the way things are done – but remember that it is only from his or her perspective. There are many variations within each culture. You will realise this when you try to explain how things are done in your culture.

Values and beliefs
1. What place does religion play in your culture
    ■ among educated/less educated people?
    ■ among men/women?
    ■ in urban/rural areas?
    ■ among older/younger people?

2. What are the main expressions of religion? (e.g. worship, festivals, processions) You may have touched on these already when you asked about festivals.

3. Is religion the main source of values for people in your culture? Where do they get their values from (e.g. parents, education, film stars, mass media, politicians, religious leaders, traditional stories, sacred books)?

4. What place does prayer have in your culture?

5. What are the most important values in your culture? (e.g. courage, sacrifice, honesty, non-violence, devotion to God, love, sincerity)

6. Is it always important to tell the truth?

REFLECTION

1. After the session, write down your reflections, as before, using the original set of questions.

2. Try to summarise your overall impression of your friend's culture – the main similarities and differences from your culture.

3. What have you learned from this experience
    ■ about your own culture?
    ■ about other cultures
    ■ about the process of developing relationships and friendship across cultures?

4. Are there any questions or areas which you would like to discuss further, either about the specific culture you have been learning about, or about the process of cross-cultural learning?

5. Reflect on your experiences in building trust. Describe how your friend was different from you, what built trust, what broke trust and what you learned about each other.

INTRODUCTION

What kind of person should I meet?

This could be the same as the person whom you interview from another cultural background. The person should, if possible, be an active follower of that faith, rather than a nominal adherent who may not know much about it. (Imagine the impression of the Christian faith which would be given by some nominal churchgoers.)

You will need to explain to your friend why you are doing this study and that this is part of your research. You will usually find that people are happy to share with you.

Purpose

The purpose, as already stated, is to listen in order to understand that faith from their perspective. It is likely that you will also share something about your own experience and faith, as the conversation develops, but that is not the primary purpose.

Developing trust and acceptance

Before you start, it is worth thinking about how you build trust with someone else. Think of a time when you failed to build trust with someone. What caused the failure? Think of people with whom you feel trust and acceptance. What makes the difference?

What obstacles keep you from making friends with people of another culture or opinion from your own? Or from going deeper with those friendships you already have? What may keep such people from making friends with you?

Think of some of the differences between you and others, (e.g. political stance, ethnic background, economic level, educational level). Now think of what you have in common, despite those differences.

In the light of all that, think of specific ways in which you can try to develop trust and acceptance with the friend you are going to interview.

GETTING STARTED

Much will depend on how well you know your friend. If you have not already spent time together, you will need to take time just to get to know each other and find out something of each other's background. Some of the introductory questions from the culture interviews will be appropriate. It is important to relate to each other primarily as people, rather than as "Hindu/ Christian". So it is worthwhile to take time to do this, in a relaxed setting. You may need to spend most of the first session for this, if this is your first proper meeting.

You can then explain again the purpose of these sessions: for you to learn about the other person's faith, in order to understand better what they

believe and why. You can say truthfully that you believe this will lead to greater understanding and respect between people of different faiths.

You can explain that you have already begun to study their faith and show them the materials, if appropriate. Ask if it will be all right to take notes, but don't do this if it becomes a distraction. Then ask them to tell you about their religious faith.

Here are four initial questions you could use:

■ What are the main observances in your faith? (E.g. worship and prayer: how often, where, alone, together?)
■ What festivals do you have?
■ What do you think God is like? How would you briefly describe Him?
■ What do you think is the purpose of the existence of human beings?

Each of these questions will lead to many more, as you ask about details of activities and their significance. Remember, your purpose is not to question why they do these things, in a critical or judging sense, though you may want to ask why in the sense of the background or purpose of a particular activity or ritual.

TAKING IT FURTHER

It is impossible to predict how your conversation will develop. It may remain at a fairly polite level or you may quickly move to a more trusting atmosphere, in which intimate beliefs and experiences can be shared and discussed.

So the questions which follow are only suggestions, which you can use in the rest of the first session and the next two. They are grouped into broad areas, which you should try to cover, though the order and the detailed questions are left to you.

God and the world
1. Where did the world come from?

2. What is the place of human beings in the world?

3. Do you believe that God is interested in each individual? In what way?

4. Do you think God has told us about himself?

5. Do you think that God intervenes in the world? How? What is the ultimate destiny of the world?

6. What do you think happens to people after death?

Perspectives on the world situation
7. What do you think about the environmental crisis? What does your faith teach about it?

8. What do you think is the cause of wars and violence? What should be the response of ordinary people?

9. Why do you think there is so much evil in the world?

10. With so much suffering in the world is it possible to believe in a loving God?

11. How would you define sin?

12. What do you believe is the worst sin?

13. Why have people of different religions fought so much in the past?

14. What do you think of the statement: "All religions are alike"?

Personal faith, prayer, spirituality

15. What does prayer mean to you?

16. Do you think God hears and answers prayer?

17. Has there been a time when God seemed close to you?

18. How can we come close to God?

19. How can God help us to deal with temptation and to overcome sin?

20. Do you think God loves us?

21. How can we obtain forgiveness?

22. Do you have a custom of asking a blessing or thanking God for a meal in your home?

Visiting a place of worship

If possible, arrange to visit a place of worship with your friend. You can then use one of the sessions to reflect on this experience together. If you cannot go together, try to arrange a visit yourself. Or you may already have visited a place of worship in the past and can talk about it with your friend.

You may have specific questions of detail arising out of your study. Or you may find that some of the questions below are useful in connection with a particular faith.

Questions Especially for Muslims

1. How do the 99 beautiful names of Allah describe him?

2. What titles are given to Jesus Christ in the holy Qur'an?

3. What does prayer mean to you?

4. Is there spiritual significance in the pilgrimage (*Hajj*)?

5. How much are you able to follow Islamic law (*Shariah*) in your daily life?

6. Do you think that keeping religious duties, such as fasting and giving alms makes a person more acceptable to Allah?

7. Does your religion make sure you will go to heaven (paradise) when you die?

Questions Especially for Hindus

1. How often do you go to the temple? How do you worship while you are there?

2. Are prayer and worship an important part of your daily life?

3. Which gods are most important to you? Why?

4. Do you read any holy books daily? If so, which one?

5. Do you expect to receive guidance from your holy books?

6. In what ways do you think we can come close to God?

7. Do you think God loves us?

RELIGION INTERVIEWS

8. Can God help us in our daily life?

9. Is it important to you to pay respect to holy men? Why?

10. Why do you think Jesus Christ died on the cross?

Questions Especially for Sikhs

1. What does the grace of God mean to you?

2. Do you meditate? If so, how?

3. How do you think God speaks to us?

4. How do you think we can become acceptable to God?

5. What makes a person commit sin? What can he do about it if he does so?

6. Were the Gurus gods or men?

7. How important to you is your family?

8. Is it important to serve our fellow men?

9. What do you believe about idols and the occult?

10. Do you know anything about Jesus Christ? If so, what?

11. Do you believe in the Holy Spirit? If so, what do you believe he can do in our lives?

REFLECTION

Spend some time in reflection after each session. Note down as much as you can remember of your friend's answers to questions.

1. What was new to you?

2. Did anything surprise you?

3. Were there any questions to which the answer seemed hard to understand or inadequate or inconsistent? Why? What does that tell you about that aspect of that faith?

4. In what way has your understanding of your friend's faith changed as a result of this session?

5. In what ways has your understanding of your own faith developed as a result of this session? (e.g. new appreciation, things that you understand more clearly, points of contrast or similarity, new questions).

6. Are there questions that you would like to discuss further:
   ■ with your friend when you next meet?
   ■ with another Christian friend?

7. Do you think you have gained in acceptance and trust? If not, what do you feel are the barriers? Perhaps areas where you still feel uneasy about each other's beliefs? Or questions which remain unanswered? If you feel there are barriers, take some time to think through the questions at the end.

8. Do you see any points of contact and communication for the Christian gospel?

9. How can you better pray for your friend? And for people of your friend's faith?

The value of reporting

If you are doing this module with supervision, you will be required to write up your period of cross-cultural experience into a report to your supervisor. Even if you are not doing the module with formal supervision, you will find it helpful to pull your learning experience together in this way; then try to find a mature Christian friend to talk it through with.

Your report should contain the following:

A   Your observations of life in the new culture, based on your notes and daily reflections. Make a summary of about 500 words, briefly describing what you did and experienced and your observations on the new culture.

B   Your personal reflection on your experience of living in that culture, how you responded to the different experiences and how you feel about your own response. Write about 1000 words. You can make use of the reflection questions in the guidelines for your interviews.

C   Your reflections on the mission of the church in that culture: as it is, as it should be. Write about 500 words.

D   Questions you would like to discuss further with your supervisor, other people with cross-cultural experience, or people of the new culture. Write down anything appropriate and discuss with your supervisor. Plan any follow up action needed.

Getting supervision

In completing this workbook, we strongly advise you to have someone who can act as a "supervisor" for you, as this will enable you to learn so much more. This needs to be a mature Christian person who has lived in another culture, preferably for two years or more. Remember that "other culture" does not have to be abroad somewhere – there are many cultural groups here in this country.

If you have someone who is willing and able to supervise you, you can send us details of this person and we will arrange for them to supervise you. Once your supervisor is approved, we will supply your supervisor with a copy of this workbook and a guide to supervising the module. They will write a brief report on you at the end of the module. The fee for this is £50. You are responsible for any expenses your supervisor may incur on your behalf. If there is a small group of you all registering for credit with the same supervisor, additional people can be registered with us for credit for £20 each.

If you need us to find and supply someone to supervise you, we will endeavour to do this through our links with different mission agencies. This may involve you in more travelling, depending on where the supervisor is. We employ and pay this person to supervise you and meet all their expenses, although you will normally be asked to travel to meet them rather than the other way round. The fee for this is £140.

Please fill in the form overleaf if you want to register for credit on either of these options. We will then take the appropriate action.

The World Christian

This workbook is for anyone wanting to learn how to take their place in the modern, international, multi-cultural, worldwide church. Enormous changes have taken place. The "cutting edge" of Christian mission has moved on from Europe and North America to other parts of the world. In some Christian circles the whole concept of cross-cultural mission is questioned.

Most of us need help to feel our way through the maze of issues involved. That is the aim of this workbook. Up-to-date facts and statistics are attractively presented. Issues are explored. Group activities and optional projects take you deeper into the subject.

The workbook covers:
- The Church around the world
- Were the missionaries mistaken?
- God's purposes for the Church
- Jesus and the Kingdom
- Key issues in mission today
- Becoming a world Christian

The World Christian has been used profitably by thousands of individuals and by many church groups. They have found it an enjoyable workbook, equipping them to begin to live their lives differently – as members of a truly worldwide church, seeking to bring the good news of Jesus to people of every culture.

Fit for the Purpose

We say that some people have a "calling". God showed them that He wanted them to be a missionary, a minister, a monk, and God opened the way for them to do so. The calling was clear, the step that needed making was clear, and they took it. Now they have a vocation.

For every Christian for whom that is true, there are dozens for whom it isn't. It's not that they love God less. It's not that they are unwilling to make sacrifices in order to serve God. They may even have some sense that God is calling them – to something. It's just that the whole thing is not that clear.

God has purposes in this world. He calls each of us to become part of them. To do that, we need to understand those purposes, and see where we fit within them. This workbook enables you to do that.

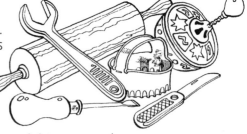

- It helps you understand the kind of life that God calls His people to live.
- It explores the place the Church has in working out God's kingdom purposes.
- It enables you to discover where you and your gifts fit in all this – including whether you might indeed become a missionary, a minister, a monk or a nun.

It also helps you become fit for that purpose. Often we need to grow in order to be the shape God needs for a particular role. If you are willing to do that, the testimony of God's people over many ages is that in pursuing God's call, with all its demands, you will find a new depth of Christian life and experience.

A4 paperbacks. £9.95. Published by St John's Extension Studies.

REGISTERING FOR SUPERVISION

Name

Address
Postcode **Telephone**

Some details about yourself, in particular why you are doing this course of study

❏ Option 1

I want to study *Entering Another's World* with supervision. I have someone nearby who can supervise me. I enclose a cheque for £50, payable to St John's College Nottingham.

Supervisor's Name

Supervisor's Address
Postcode **Telephone**

Brief description of supervisor's experience relevant to this task

❏ Option 2

I want to study *Entering Another's World* with supervision. I would like you to provide me with a supervisor. I enclose a cheque for £140, payable to St John's College Nottingham.

Signed .... Date ....

Send this form to: St John's Extension Studies, Bramcote, Nottingham NG9 3RL

FOR THE VERY KEEN

PERSPECTIVES ON THE WORLD CHRISTIAN MOVEMENT: A READER

This textbook is one of the most widely accepted and widely used mission texts available. It addresses the Biblical, Historical, Cultural and Strategic perspectives on missions, with contributions by over 70 authors.

Large format, 944 pages paperback. Published by William Carey Library, Box 41029, Pasadena, Ca. 91114, USA. Available in the UK from Paternoster Press, Box 300, Carlisle CA3 0QS. Tel: 01228 512512

The Certificate in Christian Studies

Strengthening the roots of your faith

The Certificate in Christian Studies is a practical course in applied theology, designed to equip people in every local church for ministry and mission. It is equivalent to one year of full-time study, spread over several years on a part-time basis. As a distance learning course, it is accessible throughout the UK and abroad.

A course to rely on

The CCS was established in 1978. Our current courses draw on over 20 years of experience – and it shows in the quality of our study materials, tutorial help, administration and other support. Since 1978, over 6,000 people have completed all or part of the programme.

A course of Christian development

For many different kinds of people, the CCS has been a dependable way of developing their Christian learning and discipleship.
- Many have continued to serve God where they are – giving leadership to house groups, children's and youth work, and other roles in the church.
- Others have deepened their faith and witness in the world, living out a more thoughtful Christianity in the complexities of today's society.
- Others again have been enabled to progress to further studies, sometimes for formal ministries in the church.

A national course

The number of local courses on the Christian faith has mushroomed in recent years. Local resources are necessarily limited, and the experience of students on such courses varies a great deal. By centralising the development of resources and serving a much wider Christian public, the CCS has established itself as a training course of known quality, widely accepted in many church circles. This has also helped those who have subsequently moved from one part of the country to another.

For a detailed prospectus on the Certificate in Christian Studies:

  Phone: 0115 943 6889

  Write: St John's Extension Studies, Bramcote, Nottingham NG9 3RL

  Fax: 0115 943 6438

  E-mail: ext.studies@stjohns-nottm.ac.uk

Website: www.stjohns-nottm.ac.uk